From Long Ago and Many Lands

Πάντες οἱ κατοικοῦντες
ὑπὸ τ' οὐρανοῦ ἓν γένος εἰσίν

Všichni pod oblohou jsou
jedna rodina

တ မိုယ်း အောက် တ မိ ပေါ်တ်

Under the sky
all people are
one family

WANSI WEGULU FENA
TULI BAKIKA
KIMU

天の下總ての人は一家族

மனு குலமொன்றே

كُلُّ ٱلَّذِينَ تَحْتَ ٱلسَّمَاءِ مِنْ أَهْلٍ وَاحِدٍ

His teaching was done anywhere people wanted to sit together and talk.

From Long Ago and Many Lands

Stories for Children Told Anew

by Sophia Lyon Fahs

With Teacher's Guide by Patricia Hoertdoerfer

Illustrated by Cyrus LeRoy Baldridge

Second Edition
Skinner House Books
Boston

Copyright © 1948 by Sophia Lyon Fahs and renewed 1976 by Dorothy Fahs Beck.
Teacher's Guide © 1995 by the Unitarian Universalist Association.

Published by Skinner House Books. Skinner House Books is an imprint of the
Unitarian Universalist Association, a liberal religious organization with more than
1,000 congregations in the U.S. and Canada. 25 Beacon Street, Boston, MA 02108.
All rights reserved.

This book was written before our awareness of the need for gender-inclusive
language. In a few instances, the reader may wish to change a term to one that
is inclusive of both sexes.

Printed in Canada.
ISBN 0-933840-35-7

Library of Congress Cataloging-in-Publication Data

Fahs, Sophia Blanche Lyon.
    From long ago and many lands : stories for children told anew / by Sophia Lyon
Fahs ; illustrated by Cyrus LeRoy Baldridge ; with teacher's guide by Patricia
Hoertdoerfer. — 2nd ed.
        p. cm.
Originally published: Boston : Beacon Press, 1948.
Summary: A collection of folk tales, legends, fables, and religious stories from around
the world.
    ISBN 0-933840-35-7 (alk. paper)
1. Tales. [1. Folklore.] I. Baldridge, Cyrus Leroy, 1889-1997, ill. II. Hoertdoerfer,
Pat. III. Title.
    PZ8.1.F.17 Fr 2002
    398.2   2002021671

12 11
07 06 05

Contents

Human Universals

Ideals:

Realities:

Human Diversity

Teacher's Guide

Foreword

This second edition of *From Long Ago and Many Lands* is dedicated to

Sophia Lyon Fahs
and
Florence Wolff Klaber

with profound gratitude for their leadership in liberal religious education and with deepest respect for their inspiration, challenge and legacy in Unitarian Universalist religious education.

From Long Ago and Many Lands: Stories for Children Told Anew originally was published in 1948 by Beacon Press. Reprinted six times, this collection is a classic in our liberal religious community. A small teacher's guide by Florence Wolff Klaber was also published in 1948 to supplement *From Long Ago and Many Lands.* Klaber's guide has been reprinted several times, but thirty years has lapsed since its last printing in 1962.

This second edition attempts to honor the original intent and purposes of Sophia Lyon Fahs and Florence Wolff Klaber by combining their works in one volume. These two liberal religious educators were truly pioneering leaders in many ways. They envisioned religious education as a life-long experience, integrated wisdom from many religions and cultures into their works, promoted values that are currently stated in our Purposes and Principles, nurtured a religious harmony of spirituality and ethics and cooperated across the liberal religious community in educational pursuits and publications.

Patricia Hoertdoerfer
Children's Program Director
UUA Department of Religious Education

Introduction

This second edition of *From Long Ago and Many Lands* encompasses and expresses the Principles of our Unitarian Universalist Association of Congregations, including:

The inherent worth and dignity of every person
Justice, equity and compassion in human relations
Acceptance of one another and encouragement to spiritual growth in our congregations
A free and responsible search for truth and meaning
The right of conscience and the use of the democratic process within our congregations and in society at large
The goal of world community with peace, liberty and justice for all
Respect for the interdependent web of all existence of which we are a part.

The stories in this collection are drawn from the many sources of our living tradition:

Direct experiences of that transcending mystery and wonder, affirmed in all cultures
Words and deeds of prophetic women and men
Wisdom from the world's religions
Jewish and Christian teachings
Humanist teachings
Spiritual teachings of Earth-centered traditions.

This new edition includes forty-one stories from Fahs's original collection, plus a new tale, "The Road to Olelpanti," from the Wintu Indians of North America. "The Road to Olelpanti" seemed a necessary and appropriate addition to honor Native American culture. Originally it was included in *Beginnings: Earth, Sky, Life, Death* by Fahs and Dorothy Spoerl, and they acknowledged its source from *Creation Myths of Primitive America* by Jeremiah Curtin (Boston: Little Brown and Co., 1898, pp. 163-174).

To help parents and educators introduce Fahs's work to today's children, this second edition also includes a teacher's guide for building a religious education program around these timeless tales. The guide includes story summaries and discussion questions, many of which honor the focus and original words of Florence Klaber. It is flexible and depends on teachers or parents to choose discussion questions and activities most significant and meaningful to their particular child, class and congregation, and to their teaching style and skills.

The stories in this collection are a treasury of folktale, scripture and children's literature culled from many ages and civilizations. They illustrate basic and universal themes that are of the deepest significance to a child's religious development.

When writing the original edition of *From Long Ago and Many Lands*, Fahs drew her stories from a "wide variety of cultures, races and religions." She wanted children to celebrate "the human universals that bind us together in a common world of brotherhood [humanity]." Fahs's stories are not primarily concerned with Jewish, Christian, Islamic, Buddhist, Hindu or Confucian beliefs. Nor do they focus on the history of specific ethnic groups or cultures, such as Greek, German, Arab, Ugandan, Japanese or Native American. The focus is on individuals in the human family who have had challenging experiences. In many stories the solution is satisfying. In other cases, there is much room for diverse opinions and alternative viewpoints. At times we may disagree or not approve of the choices made by characters in the story. That is good.

These stories are not presented as final pronouncements or static rules to live by, but as tools to stimulate thought, evaluation and "new" perspective. *From Long Ago and Many Lands* is a guide book that may be used to help children think through their own problems in life situations and human relations. It can also teach them to appreciate the universality of ethical problems and the diverse ways people search for satisfying solutions to these problems.

Fahs originally chose the stories in this collection for the enjoyment and comprehension they would bring to children ages 7 to 9. Parents can tell these stories at bedtime; leaders can use these stories in children's worship or intergenerational worship services; and teachers can tell these stories in religious education classes when considering some of life's universal questions, discussing the wonder of birth or the mystery of death, exploring human ideals, focusing on specific real life issues or celebrating ways to live together.

The stories in this second edition have been rearranged into four units. The first half of the book depicts humanity's yearning and search for an overall philosophy of life. These stories address the abiding questions that old and young alike ask about the mysteries of life, death and god.

The stories in the last half of the book deal with human relationships and explore such values as fairness, cooperation, honesty, friendship, freedom, responsibility and respect. They are concerned with the home and kinship, with how people should live with one another.

In our life journey, we search for truths to give ultimate meaning and purpose to life and the forces that control the universe. Intuitively and intellectually we strive to work with the order and rhythm that is the essence of all. This search and desire has flowered into religion as we generally understand it. In our schools of religion and religious education programs we desire to encourage this yearning and this searching. We want our children to seek and to discover the eternal truths for themselves. Our faith is in the journeying, alone and together, with people through the ages and with people yet to come, who have similar hopes and aspirations.

Introduction to the First Edition

"What has happened to yesterday? And where did today come from?" asked four-year-old Peter in an unexpectedly thoughtful moment. I wanted to tell him that yesterday had not gone. It is still living inside today in much the same way that the acorn lives inside the oak tree.

But Peter would not have understood me. Nor would I have really understood my own words. Peter and I together stand in awe before the mystery of Time. But Peter's yesterdays to me seem few in number. His imagination does not yet go beyond his own personal experiences. Some day Peter will be surprised to learn that there were yesterdays before he was born. Later on, he will feel his wisdom growing as he tries to stretch his mind to the yesterdays before his father and his grandfather were born. When Peter goes to school it will slowly dawn upon his imagination that the marching line of yesterdays reaches back and back into centuries and millenniums.

This collection of stories has been made as a kind of pre-history for children of seven, eight and nine, whose feelings for the long, long ago are still vague, but stretching. Before children learn historical facts and dates, we think it desirable that they discover through such simple tales as these that the people of long ago were real and that in the deepest and most important ways they were like the people of today. We only wish we were more thoroughly acquainted with the world's literature so that the collection might have been even more representative.

In selecting these stories out of the vast treasury of ancient folklore, legend and history, we have had a few fundamental principles to guide our choices. Parents and teachers who will tell or read these stories to their children may wish to know these guiding principles.

First, we have chosen stories having the kind of narrative that, in our judgment, children from seven to nine will enjoy. We realize, or course, that children much older will like these stories perhaps equally well, yet we have excluded from this book all stories that we regard as beyond the understanding and the experiences of this younger group.

We decided also that the stories chosen should be more than interesting. In some pertinent manner, they should bear on the children's own living. Their own experiences and those told them from the long ago should be like two opposite currents of electricity. They should be different enough to attract each other, and yet fundamentally they should be so much alike that when they are brought near together a spark is born that unites the two into one common experience.

Another important principle has been to choose stories from a wide variety of different cultures, races and religions so that early in life children may begin to feel some of the human universals that bind us together in a common world kinship. Our finest moral and spiritual ideals have been shared by many peoples.

The emphasizing of ideals, however, has not led us to discard stories merely because they picture life's tragedies and evils. None of the people described in these stories should be presented as perfect. Children should know at an early age that all humans are imperfect. Learning from the past should mean learning by one's mistakes as well as by one's achievements.

Again, we have intentionally excluded from this collection stories telling of divine, miraculous interventions in the affairs of people, involving the setting aside of known laws of the natural world. This principle has led to the exclusion of myths of gods and goddesses. It has led also to the omission of many stories from the bibles of Jews and Christians, commonly told to young children of the West, as well as similar stories found in the bibles of other religions. This we have done because, in our judgment, the telling of miracle stories is more likely to complicate the problems of life for young children than to bring them enlightenment. Such stories are usually either accepted as factual by young children or else seem utterly unbelievable. If the first result follows, children are given an unrealistic conception of the universe — one which is contrary to the general assumptions of a scientific age. If children think the stories are unbelievable, they may gain the impression that all religious beliefs belong to a fairy world.

We have made three exceptions in the application of this principle regarding miracle stories, for we have included the stories of the miraculous births of Jesus, Buddha and Confucius. This has been done because, in the present stage of cultural development in the West, it seems to be practically impossible to protect young children from hearing the story of the miraculous birth of Jesus. During the Christmas season this story is told and retold in storybooks, pictures and carols.

In our manner of telling the story of the birth of Jesus, however, we have tried to give some understanding of how the story first came to be told, and in addition we have placed it alongside the stories of the miraculous births of Buddha and Confucius. With the three stories side by side, it is hoped that children may be given a broader understanding which will enable them to think for themselves. This should be possible, at least for those children who have already been told some of the scientific facts regarding the birth of babies. We hope that the result will not be merely a negative disbelief; that it may rather be a new appreciation of the significance to humankind of a truly great person and a realization that all people everywhere feel touched by an unutterable mystery when in the presence of a newborn babe.

The exclusion of miraculous stories in general has led also to the exclusion of stories of witches and fairies who can do magic. For this book and for these younger children we are of the opinion that such stories are not the best. This seems especially so when the idea of magic is linked with ideas of good and evil — when the good child is magically rewarded and the bad child is punished. We do not care to encourage young children to wish for magical help out of difficulties, nor do we wish to frighten them by picturing unreal forms of punishment. When children are a little older than eight or nine they may be able to accept such fairy tales of magic as symbolic of common fears, wishes and ethical standards, and sense the true meanings in the stories.

This collection, however, does contain a number of fanciful tales. Some have a generous touch of humor in them. But these are, for the most part, fables, such as the Jataka stories from India and Aesop's fables from Greece. In these stories young children can recognize the fancifulness and will not mistake it for fact. The help given in these stories by one animal to another is seldom the magical help of a fairy, but rather the kind of help that one human being may give to another.

So it is that these stories have been chosen with quite definite principles in mind. On the one hand, we have deleted from the book old stories that seem to have no valuable meaning. On the other hand, we hope that no tale in the book will be told primarily to teach a moral. These stories represent the thoughts of people of long ago. The characters in them are not heroes whose actions are to be copied. They are those who, long ago, experimented with new ways of living. Always the child's own thoughts should be encouraged. That we should think differently sometimes from even the best of those of long ago should never be a surprise.

SOPHIA LYON FAHS

June 1, 1948

To Story Writers — Ancient and Modern

There is nothing original in this book except the choice of the stories put into the volume and the author's own imaginative touches, introduced to make the action of the stories vivid and convincing for the children who read them.

All the stories in the book are old. Probably none is less than four hundred years old, while more than half of the forty-one tales come from the centuries before the birth of Christ. These stories, therefore, have been told by word of mouth, or have been passed on in written form on stone or palm leaves or parchment or on the printed page, over and over again. They represent, in their original telling, a dozen or more languages. Some have been translated into hundreds of other languages and dialects. It is clearly impossible, therefore, to say definitely who is the original author of any given story.

In all cases I have sought to go back of any recent popular rendering of the story for children to find a source as close to the original written form as possible. In no case has the translation or source been merely copied. I have assumed that the structure of these ancient tales has long since become our common heritage. The adaptations here made in the telling are the author's own.

Almost a fourth of the stories in this collection, so far as I know, have never before been written for English-speaking children. These are the historical story of King Asoka of India, entitled "The King Who Changed His Mind"; the Chinese story, "A Visit to the Land-of-Great-Men"; the ancient tale about Buddha entitled "The Mustard-Seed Medicine"; the other three stories from the ancient Buddhist scriptures entitled "The Questions of King Milinda," "A Musician and His Trumpet" and "The Dog and the Heartless King"; the two miracle stories of

"The Birth of Buddha" and "The Birth of Confucius"; and the two oldest stories of the entire collection, found in the ancient Upanishads of India, entitled "The Fig Seed" and "The Lump of Salt."

I owe my discovery of the two stories from the Upanishads, entitled "The Fig Seed" and "The Lump of Salt," to the late Dr. Robert E. Hume, who translated the stories to me orally one afternoon directly from the Sanskrit, using simpler terminology than he had used in his scholarly book, *The Thirteen Principal Upanishads, Translated from the Sanskrit* (Oxford University Press, 1921). The syllable "shad" in the word "Upanishad" is from the root meaning "to sit down." "Upan" and "ni" are prepositions. The name, therefore, denotes discussions held between a teacher and his followers while they are sitting together. Svetakatu and his father, Vaj-na-val-kya, the characters in the two stories chosen here, are now regarded as historical characters of considerable renown in ancient Vedic India. The Upanishads are to the modern Brahman what the New Testament is to the Christian, and were written sometime before the sixth century B.C.

"The Mustard-Seed Medicine," "A Musician and His Trumpet," "The Questions of King Milinda" and "The Blind Men and the Elephant" are all found in ancient volumes of the Buddhist scriptures. The best English source for these four stories probably is *Buddhist Parables,* translated from the original Pali by E. W. Burlingame (Yale University Press, 1922).

The Jataka are stories supposedly told by Buddha himself, in each of which he relates some experience from one of his previous existences before he finally attained Enlightenment. There are in all five hundred and fifty of the Jataka, or birth stories. I have chosen but four: "The Dog and the Heartless King," "The Nervous Little Rabbit," "The Two Friends" and "The Old Bowl." Many of these stories are thought to be older than Buddha's time. After his death they were collected and all were linked to the name of the saint. The Jataka have been called "the oldest, most complete and most important collection of folklore extant."

A complete collection of these stories is contained in *The*

Jataka, Being Tales of the Anterior Births of Gotama Buddha, for the first time edited in the original Pāli by V. Fausböll (Trubner and Company, 1877-1897).

Another source is *The Jataka or Stories of the Buddha's Former Births,* translated from the Pāli by various hands, edited by E. B. Cowell (Cambridge University Press, 1895-1907).

The three fables, "The Complaint against the Stomach," "The Wind and the Sun" and "The Miller, His Boy and Their Donkey," are all from the well-known fables attributed to Aesop, a Greek who lived from about 620 to 560 B.C. The classic children's book in which the best of these Aesop's fables have been collected is *The Fables of Aesop,* edited by Joseph Jacobs (The Macmillan Company, 1894).

Information regarding King Asoka was gathered principally from the following: *Asoka* by D. R. Bhandarbar (University of Calcutta Press, 1925); *Asoka, The Buddhist Emperor of India* by Vincent A. Smith (3rd ed.; Clarendon Press, 1920); and *The Indian Gods and Kings* by Emma Hawkridge (Houghton Mifflin Company, 1935). Photographic prints of the Asoka pillars and inscriptions can be found in *Archaeological Survey of Northern India* by A. Führer (W. H. Allen and Company, 1897).

The original renderings of the stories from the Hebrew and Christian Bible can be found in the following passages: "The Trees Choose a King," Judges 9:1-15; "King Saul Finds a Harpist," I Samuel 16:14-23 and 18:1-29; "David and Jonathan Become Friends," I Samuel 19:1-10 and 20:1-42; "The King's Spear and Water Jug," I Samuel 22:1-2 and 26:1-25; and "Wise King Solomon," I Kings 3:4-28.

The original renderings of the stories from the New Testament can be found in the following passages: "The Jewish Traveler and the Robbers," Luke 10:25-37; "The Very Short Rule," Matthew 7:12, Luke 6:31, Mark 7:1-5 and 14-23 (the reference to standing on one foot was taken from a Jewish legend about Rabbi Hillel, found in *Studies in Pharisaism and the Gospels* by Israel Abrahams, Cambridge University Press, 1942); "Jesus at a Wedding Party," Luke 6:32-36 and 14:7-14; "The Birth of Jesus," Matthew 2:1-12, Luke 1:26-38 and 2:1-20.

The details included in the story of "The Birth of Buddha" and in the story entitled "Gautama Finds Out for Himself" may be found in *Buddhist Birth Stories,* translated from the Pali by V. Fausböll and edited by T. W. Davids (Houghton Mifflin Company, 1880), and in *The Gospel of Buddha* by Paul Carus (Open Court Publishing Company, 1915).

The Greek historical legend entitled "The Richest King in the World" may be found in any English translation of the works of Herodotus (Book i, the section entitled "Clio"). Herodotus lived in the fifth century B.C. Solon was the ruler of Athens, and Croesus was king of Lydia in Asia Minor. These two both lived in the time of Cyrus the Great who ruled during the sixth century B.C.

The other Greek historical legend, entitled "Damon and Pythias," may be found in the *Parallel Lives* written by Plutarch, that great Greek biographer who lived from about 46 to 125 A.D. It was also told by Cicero. There are a number of good English translations of Plutarch's *Lives.* The story is found in his life of Dionysius, the tyrannical ruler of Syracuse, who lived from 432 to 367 B.C. The version of the story used in this book was written especially for this volume by Mrs. Florence W. Klaber.

A translation of the Chinese story of "A Visit to the Land-of-Great-Men" may be found in *Gems of Chinese Literature,* translated by Herbert A. Giles (Benn Brothers, Ltd., 1923). It comes originally from the *Ching Hua Yuan,* a Chinese book of the seventeenth century A.D.

The story of "The Birth of Confucius" is based largely upon a book containing translations of Chinese inscriptions and stone rubbings of pictorial art on a series of stone tablets that are in the Holy Shrine at Confucius' birthplace. The book is entitled *The Life of Confucius* (Kwang Hsueh Publishing House, China agency for the Oxford University Press, no date).

"The Bell of Atri" is a retelling of the poem of the same name to be found in the works of Henry W. Longfellow.

"The Naumburg Children's Festival" was discovered in *Bedford's Manual* of 1884-85, and also in a paper-bound booklet written in German, *Naumburger Kirschfest* by Waldemar D. Nachf (N. Seiling Pub., 1924).

In the following instances, being unable to find earlier and more original sources, I am indebted to specific authors and publishers for the structure of the stories used. I therefore wish to express special thanks to them for their kind permission to use certain material:

For "The Boy Who Was Afraid to Try" and "The Two Cheats," to *The King of the Snakes* by Rosetta Baskerville (Church Missionary Society, 1922).

For "The Blind Man and the Lame Man," to *The Flame Tree* by Rosetta Baskerville (Church Missionary Society, no date).

For "A Ring-around of Temper," to *Stories from the Early World* by R. M. Fleming (Benn Brothers, Ltd., 1922).

For "The Whale and the Big Bronze Statue," to *Tales from Old Japan* by Allen Leslie Whitehorn (Frederick A. Stokes, no date).

For "The Wee, Wise Bird," to *Stories from the Rabbis* by Abraham Isaacs (Charles Webster and Company, 1893).

For "The Camel Driver in Need of a Friend," to *Folklore of the Holy Land* by J. E. Hanauer (Duckworth and Company, 1907).

For "Who Ate the Squabs?" to *The Shepherd and the Dragon, Fairy Tales from the Czech*, translated by Eleanor E. Ledbetter (Robert M. McBride Company, 1930).

For "The Picture on the Kitchen Wall," to *Tales of a Chinese Grandmother* by Frances Carpenter (Doubleday and Company, 1937); I owe to this version the combining of the characters of the Kitchen God and the historical person of Chang Hung.

For "The Persevering Ant," to Elsie Spicer Eells; the story appeared in *John Martin's Book,* January, 1916 (Doubleday and Company).

In addition to these writers and publishers, I am deeply grateful to a number of friends who have helpfully influenced the choices of stories. The Reverend Ernest W. Kuebler, Director of the Division of Education of the American Unitarian Association, and the Committee on Curriculum and Worship, with whom I am continually working, have examined the manuscript and given many valuable suggestions. The members of the committee are as follows: Raymond B. Johnson, Chairman; Susan M. Andrews, Executive Director of Religious Education in the Universalist Church; Walter G. Couch; Florence W. Klaber; Marguerite Hallowell, Office Secretary of the Philadelphia Yearly Meeting of Friends; Elizabeth M. Manwell; Helen M. Robertson; and Dorothy T. Spoerl. The late Mrs. Karl Chworowsky was also a member of this committee.

Dr. D. Willard Lyon, my brother, formerly Secretary of the National Y.M.C.A. in China, helped me to discover some of the stories from China. My sister, Mrs. Charles H. Lyon, and my daughter, Mrs. Lois Fahs Timmins, have also given me valuable editorial assistance.

To all these and to others who have encouraged the project I am most grateful.

S.L.F.

The End Papers

The proverb written in different languages on the beginning and end papers of this book reads in English, "Under the sky all people are one family." This is an old Chinese proverb—as old as the stories in this collection. Other peoples and cultures have used the same or similar proverbs or expressions, thus, the fifteen different translations in this book.

The prevailing theme in all these stories is that everyone around the world is related to everyone else. In fact, all of us are so much alike that our world becomes a global village and we are all sisters and brothers in the human family.

Here is a puzzle for you!
Whenever you read or hear one of these stories, see if you can find the language in which that story was first told. Here are a few hints.

The animal stories from India and the stories of Buddha and Asoka may have been told either in Tamil or Urdu. The very, very old stories of the wise men of India were once written in Sanskrit. Jesus spoke in Aramaic. King Solomon spoke in Hebrew. The man who first wrote the story from the Indians of Brazil probably wrote in Portuguese; and the Africans of Uganda talked in Baganda.

This diagram will show you what the languages are and where to find them.

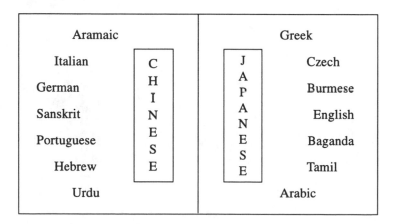

The Abiding Questions

The Picture on the Kitchen Wall

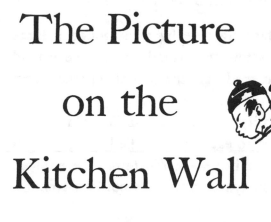

A Story from China

Long, long ago in the land of China there lived a very old grandfather, named Chang Kung, who had a very large family. First, there were Chang Kung's own sons. When his sons grew up they all married and their wives came to live in Chang Kung's house. Then grandchildren were born. When these grandsons grew up, they also married and their wives were added to Chang Kung's family. Then came the great-grandchildren. So Chang Kung's family grew and grew until there were several hundred people in it — all living together. There were old people and young people, middle-sized people and children. Always there were a number of babies.

Besides all this, Chang Kung's family was very fond of pet animals, especially dogs. It is said that at one time one hundred pet dogs belonged to the household.

As Chang Kung's family grew larger and larger, his house had to grow bigger and bigger too, until it became a

3

collection of houses standing side by side around a large open courtyard. A high stone wall stood like a fence around all the houses, and that made all the houses together seem like one big home.

The larger his family grew, the happier old Chang Kung became. He liked to eat at one of the big long tables with his big and little children beside him. He enjoyed sitting in the sunny courtyard where he could watch his great-grandchildren play.

But Chang Kung's family is not remembered after these many years simply because it was such a large family. Many people of China have large families. Chang Kung is still remembered because, it is said, the members of his family *never quarreled*. At least so the story goes. The children never quarreled in their play. The old people never quarreled with each other and never scolded the children. Nobody — big or little — ever said a cross word. Nobody ever did a mean thing. Some said jokingly that even the dogs did not quarrel or bite. When they were brought their bones they would not even bark, but all would wag their tails and wait their turns!

Stories about this remarkable household spread far and wide over the country just as the breezes blow far and wide in the spring. Finally news of Chang Kung's happy family reached the ears of the Emperor.

Now it so happened that the Emperor was about to make a journey to the Western Hills, to a place not far from the home of Chang Kung. So he decided to visit this wonderful household on his way back, and to see for himself whether or not the rumors he had heard were true.

What a sight it was the day the Emperor arrived outside

the village gate! First in the royal procession came the very tall guards dressed in blue and red, carrying long bows and arrows in their hands. Then came the mandarins, those important men in the Emperor's court. Their long silk gowns were beautifully embroidered with figures of colored birds. Blue and green peacock feathers waved from their round hats. Other attendants followed, playing flutes and harps as the procession marched down the street.

At last came the Emperor himself in his richly adorned sedan chair, carried on the shoulders of four men in red. When the Emperor entered the gate of Chang Kung's home, the old man himself was there to bow many times and to greet his Emperor with very polite words.

"Very excellent and very aged Sir," said the Emperor, "it is said that inside your walls no cross words are ever spoken. Can this be true?"

"Lord of ten thousand years," said Chang Kung, "you do my poor house far too much honor. It is true that my family does not quarrel, but it would please us greatly if you would consent to walk about our humble courts and judge for yourself."

So the Emperor made his way from one house to another

and from one room to another. He talked with everyone he met. In the great Hall of Politeness, he was served delicious food and drink. As he sipped his tea from a dainty cup, he said to Chang Kung: "You must have a golden secret in order to keep so many people living together in such order and peace. I, too, should like to know your secret."

Then old Chang Kung called his servants to bring a tablet of smooth bamboo. (In those long-ago days there was no paper. All writing was done on wood or on stone.) Chang Kung asked also for his brush and ink, and the ink-stone with its little well of water. He took the brush in his hand and, dipping it into the water and then on the ink, he wrote one word on the tablet. He wrote the word a second time and a third time. He wrote the word over and over until he had written it one hundred times. Then with a low bow, he placed the tablet in the hands of the Emperor.

"You have written many words," said the Emperor, "but at the same time you have written only one word."

"Ai, ai," said Chang Kung, "but that one word *is* the golden secret, O Son of Heaven. It is KINDNESS over and over without any ending." Chang Kung nodded his gray head as he spoke.

The Emperor was so pleased with the golden secret that he, too, called for a bamboo tablet. Taking the brush that Chang Kung had used, the Emperor wrote these words on his tablet: "Let all the families of China learn the golden secret of Chang Kung and his family."

When the Emperor had finished writing, he said: "Let this tablet be fastened to the outside of the gate where everyone passing may read it."

Not many years after the Emperor's visit Chang Kung died, but the story of his happy household has never been forgotten. People asked the Emperor to have pictures of the old man painted and sold so that families might hang his picture on the wall above their kitchen stoves to remind them to keep the golden secret that Chang Kung and his family had learned.

That is why, after these many, many years, in thousands of homes in China, at the New Year season, a fresh bright

picture of Chang Kung is pasted on the wall behind the kitchen stove. Many Chinese will tell you it is a picture of a god, but you should know that Chang Kung was once just a very kind and good man who helped the members of his family to learn to live happily together without quarreling. Since so many people think that God is perhaps much like the very best person that can be imagined, such a good person as Chang Kung seems to them to be like God himself.

To look at the picture of Chang Kung over the kitchen stove every morning helps to remind many thousands of people in China to speak kindly to one another. They feel as if Chang Kung were watching them and listening as they go about their work. They can sometimes imagine they hear him speak that golden word — KINDNESS.

Once a year on the night before New Year's, the picture of Chang Kung is taken down and burned. As the flames and smoke go upward, the people think: "Chang Kung is flying back to heaven to tell the great God of all the people just how well everyone has behaved during the past year."

Three days later, they will paste new pictures of Chang Kung on the walls over their kitchen stoves and they will say: "He has now come back again to the earth to keep watch over us for another year."

The Jewish Traveler and the Robbers

A Story from Palestine

THIS IS A STORY that Jesus told a very long time ago. Some of those who used to go to Jesus to learn from him were apt to be very particular about the kinds of people they were good to. This story told them what Jesus thought about the way they acted. It told them without his saying it right out in just so many words.

Very early one morning just as it was beginning to grow light, a Jewish merchant rose from the mat on which he had been sleeping. He rubbed his eyes and called: "Wife, it is time for us to wake up. I must be on my way. It is a good five hours to Jericho. I want to get as far as I can in the cool of the morning. The scorching sun on that Jericho road is almost more than I can bear."

So, with his wife's help, the Jewish merchant soon had two big bundles of the goods he was to sell strapped to his donkey's back, and off he and his donkey jogged down the

9

narrow street in front of his house and out toward the big gate in the city wall.

As he came near the gate, the merchant stopped to speak to the man on guard. "Good morning, sir!" he said.

"And good morning to you!" called the guard at the gate as he swung open the heavy wooden door.

"Where are you bound so early in the morning?" asked the guard.

"To Jericho, to sell my goods."

"Are you not afraid to go alone, sir?" asked the guard. "The road to Jericho is dangerous. Robbers hide in the bushes along the cliffs. I am told they have lately been very rough with travelers. Ride fast, sir, when you come to those sudden bends in the road."

"Thank you, good friend. I've often gone over this road alone, and I have never yet been harmed."

"May you be spared once again!" called the guard.

The air was crisp and fresh. In the fields along the road bright red poppies bloomed. The merchant liked the perfume of the orange and lemon blossoms. The olive trees in the orchards along the way seemed like old friends. Now and then as the rider and donkey passed some square stone house, the owner would bow and say "Good morning!" or a child playing in the grass would wave to the traveler and smile.

As the merchant rode on, the air began to grow warmer. The sun rising higher in the sky shone brighter and hotter. After a while there were no longer any pleasant olive groves or orange trees or houses or people. The mountainsides were hard and dry and covered with rocks. The road was steep and wound around the edges of cliffs. The dwarf trees were sharp with thorns, and brown with dried leaves. For a long time the merchant saw no other travelers. He remembered the warning of the guard at the gate. He grasped his stick more tightly and urged the donkey on.

Suddenly, without any warning, three robbers sprang from behind a clump of bushes. Almost before the merchant knew what was happening to him, they pounced upon him, pulled him off his donkey, snatched his stick away and threw him on the ground. They pulled his money bag from his belt, took his water bottle from his side, and stripped off most of his clothes. Then they hit him on his back and head with their sticks until he was so cut he began to bleed, and until the poor man was too injured to feel the pain any longer. They dragged him to the side of the road and left him as if he were dead.

Then off the robbers went with the merchant's donkey and his two big bundles of goods.

How long the poor merchant lay beside the road in the glare of the sun he never knew. When finally he awakened, his head was aching and his whole body was so sore and tired he could not move. He wanted to crawl over under the shadow of a rock near by, but it was so painful to move he could only lie still. His throat felt dry. He panted for breath. He had never in all his life wanted so much to have just one little sip of cool water.

As he lay alone and helpless, he wondered what he could do. He listened eagerly for the sound of footsteps either up or down the road. "If only some traveler would come along," he thought. But the place was very still. All he could hear was the buzzing of insects in his ears. He waited, half asleep.

Finally, he thought he heard a faint sound far off in the distance. Klick, klick, klickity, klick. The sick man opened his eyes. He tried to look down the road. But he could not raise his head. The sound seemed to come nearer. It grew louder. Klick, klick, klickity, klick.

At last at the bend in the road, he saw a man on a donkey riding up the road toward him. The man was richly dressed. Blue tassels hung from his shawl. "I hope he is a good man," thought the Jewish merchant.

He raised one of his hands a few inches. "Water, water," he called faintly. The man halted his donkey. He looked over toward the side of the road. Then he gave a frightened glance at the cliff above. "Oh dear, oh dear," he murmured. "Robbers have been here. I must hurry on or else I, too, will be robbed and beaten." So he struck his donkey with his stick and off he rode. The patter of hoofs grew fainter and fainter until they died away entirely.

Again the helpless merchant could hear only the buzzing of insects in his ears. The hot sun blazed down on his
almost naked body. His throat became dryer and dryer.
Soon he felt so tired and sore that he stopped feeling anything at all.

After another long while, he was awakened. Klick,
klick, klickity, klick. It was dim at first, then slowly grew
plainer and plainer. The sick man began again to be hope-
ful. He would call louder this time. Surely this traveler
would stop and help him.

When the traveler and the donkey came near enough,
the sick man noticed some cymbals hanging at the donkey's
side. "He is a good man," thought the merchant. "He is
a musician who plays in the temple. Surely he will stop and
help me."

"Water! Water!" he called as loudly as he could.

The traveler stopped his donkey and started to dismount.
Then he changed his mind and remounted. He struck the
donkey sharply with his stick and off he rode. "That man
is almost dead. If I help him he may die on my hands.
Then what would I do? And besides I must be in Jerusalem
before sunset." Klick, klick, klickity, klick went the donkey's hoofs in the direction of the big city.

Again all was quiet on the lonely road. The merchant
once more fell asleep from weakness. When a third traveler came by, the sick man was too weak to hear the sound
of the donkey's trot. He could not speak or turn his head
to look. He lay as if he were dead. He did not even know
when the kind arms lifted his head and poured a little cool
wine between his parched lips. Perhaps it was just as well
he did not hear the traveler talking to himself.

"Shall I help him or not?" the traveler muttered as he stood looking down on the helpless man. "He's a Jew and I am a despised foreigner — a Samaritan. If he were well and I were helpless in his place would he help me? Jews won't even speak to my people. How many times I have been jeered at by Jewish boys and have been called names as if I were an animal. How they have snapped out the word Samaritan at me as if I were poison! But this man is dying. He may have some children who need him and a wife who loves him. I'm going to do for him what I wish he would do for me if I am ever as helpless as he is."

So this Samaritan traveler took water from his own water bottle and bathed the man's hot face and hands. He took oil from another bottle and poured it tenderly on the bleeding parts. Then he tore strips off his own clothes and wrapped the pieces around the man's bleeding arms and head.

At last the Jewish merchant opened his eyes. He looked up at the kind face that was smiling down at him. Soon he was sitting slumped over on the back of the stranger's donkey, and his new-found friend was walking beside him and holding him to keep him from falling as they went down the steep and winding road.

At last they reached the green and pleasant plain. Ahead was a wayside inn where travelers might stop for a night's rest and food. The good friend tenderly lifted the helpless man off the donkey and carried him to a little room. He spread out his own sleeping mat, laid the man down and made him as comfortable as he could. All through the night, the stranger lay beside the sick man and cared for him.

When morning came, the Jewish merchant was feeling much better, but he was still too sore and weak to walk. "I think you will soon be well again," said his new-found friend. Then the stranger called the keeper of the inn into the room and said:

"Here is some money to pay for whatever care this man needs until he is well enough to go home. If he needs to stay longer than this money will pay for, just let me know the next time I come around and I will pay the rest."

And this is the story that Jesus told his followers.

The Dog
and the
Heartless King

A Story from India

ONCE UPON A TIME there lived a King who cared for nobody but himself. He had grown rich from the high taxes he had forced his people to pay, while they had become poorer and poorer. He lived in a gorgeous palace, while the poor men who built it for him still lived in thatched huts and tumble-down hovels. The King's table was always heaped with delicious foods, while most of his people had only one plain meal a day, and sometimes not even that. But the heartless king did not care. If he had what *he* wanted, that was enough for him to think about.

One day a hunter came to the palace gate, intending to teach the heartless King a lesson. The hunter brought with him an enormous dog. The King was fond of hunting and this enormous dog fascinated him. So the man and dog were both welcomed into the palace grounds.

But the enormous dog was no ordinary dog, and his bark was like the roar of thunder. The first time he opened his

16

big mouth and barked, the awful noise shook the walls of the palace and frightened the King and all his courtiers. If the dog had stopped with one or two barks, the matter might have been forgotten.

But again and again his fierce roaring shook the earth. Before long there was no resting between barks. Nobody in the palace could hear himself talk. The King was desperate and sent for the hunter. He asked:

"Why does your dog make such a deafening noise?"

"The dog is hungry," said the hunter.

Immediately the King ordered that a big plateful of meat be brought. In almost no time at all the enormous dog licked the plate clean. Then at once he began barking again.

A second plateful of meat was brought. This was disposed of just as quickly as the first. Again the dog began barking.

Over and over the plate was filled, and over and over the enormous dog quickly made away with the whole plateful and began barking as loudly as ever. The King was angry. He called the hunter and said:

"You and your dog must leave the palace at once. We cannot endure this deafening noise any longer." But the hunter was firm.

"Your Majesty, we have been sent to you by One greater than you are. We are here to stay." The King was frightened. He grasped the arms of his chair and stared at the hunter. The King was not accustomed to having anyone speak to him in this manner.

"Will nothing satisfy the hunger of your enormous dog?" he said at last.

"Nothing that is easy for you to give. He might be

satisfied if he were given the flesh of his enemies to eat."

"Who are the dog's enemies?" asked the King in surprise.

"Those who are keeping the people of this country always hungry. Those who are eating all the food there is, and who are not dividing it with those who do the work in the fields to make the food grow. Your Majesty, so long as there are any people in your kingdom who are kept hungry this dog will bark."

On hearing the hunter say this, the King was even more frightened than ever. It had never before entered his thoughts that he had been doing anything wrong. He had supposed that the people of his kingdom should always do exactly what he wanted. It had never occurred to him that a King should think of the happiness of anyone except himself.

He was now angry from his head to his feet, inside and outside. Either he would go mad hearing the continuous barking of that enormous dog, or else something would have to be done and that very quickly. So he called his wise men together and said: "What shall I do?"

The wise men bowed their heads and walked off to think over the question together. But try as hard as they could, they could see only two possible things to do. Either the enormous dog must be killed or else every hungry person in the kingdom must be fed. No one of them was courageous enough to offer to kill the dog. So that meant there was only one thing left to do. Everybody in the kingdom must somehow be fed. The wise men were very clear in their minds about it. They returned to the King and told him plainly what had to be done. The King hesitated no longer.

"Put all the servants on the palace grounds to work at once!" he commanded. "Go to the storerooms and get all the bags of rice you can find. Pile them high on carts. Take also meat from my cupboards and gather vegetables and fruits from my gardens. Send men out with these loaded carts into all the towns and villages in my kingdom. Command my servants to find all the people who are hungry. Give them generously of these foods until not a single man, woman or child in the land is hungry."

The wise men hurried away to do as their King commanded. Soon there was shouting and laughing, hustling and bustling all over the palace. In fact, the royal servants made so much noise that they forgot to listen to the barking of the enormous dog. Presently a long line of carts, piled high with bags and baskets of food, rolled out through the palace gate. All day long and day after day the carts kept going until they had gone to every village in the land and until food was taken to every house where somebody was hungry.

At last the day came when the enormous dog really stopped barking and lay down quietly beside the King's chair. The dog was satisfied. All the people inside the palace ground were happy and at peace in their minds. Everywhere in the land everybody was contented.

The heartless King had learned his lesson.

The Very Short Rule

A Story from Palestine

WHEN JESUS CAME INTO TOWN, someone who knew him was sure to pass the word around. A plan would be worked out for him to be at a certain place when evening came and the day's work was done. Then men and women who had to work during the day could gather and listen to what Jesus had to say.

Sometimes they would find him in the house of a friend. And the number of people who would come might fill the whole house and the street outside, too. Other times they would follow Jesus to the lake. He and some of his fishermen friends would step into a boat. They would anchor it near the shore. The people would sit on the rocks and grass near by, and Jesus would stand up in the boat and talk to everybody.

Often they would go home after listening to Jesus, and they would remember just one little story or one short sentence that Jesus had said. But that little bit they remembered a long, long time, because somehow they liked to remember it.

Sometimes there were men and women who listened to Jesus who were very much discouraged. Some were so poor they did not get enough to eat. Some had sick children to take care of at home. Some were old and crippled and always in pain. Some felt that nobody cared for them. They were always given the meanest jobs to do and they were always being scolded because they did not do them well enough.

There were others who felt it was scarcely worth while trying to be good at all. No one was ever pleased with what they did no matter how hard they tried.

These people went regularly once a week to the synagogue [1] on the Sabbath.[2] They heard the Bible read to them, but they could not remember all that they heard, so they did not do all that they were told they ought to do. They knew they were not praying as often as they were told to pray, but it was so hard to remember the words to say. They knew they were not giving as much as they were told to give to the synagogue, but they had so little to live on, how could they give more? They admitted that they did some work on the Sabbath while the teachers said they should never do any work at all on that day. But the hours in the week were not long enough to get everything done that had to be done to keep the children from starving.

Such people as these were naturally discouraged. They felt all the time that their teachers were not pleased with them. If their teachers were not pleased, then probably

---

[1] The Jewish name for church.
[2] The Sabbath is the Jewish Sunday.

God was not pleased either. This thought made them feel even more discouraged.

One day as Jesus was sitting in a boat and the people were squatting on the rocks along the shore, one of these discouraged men asked a question.

"I am a shepherd," he said. "I have to spend long hours in the open fields. When eating time comes, I cannot always find a brook where I can wash my hands before I eat. It is the rule, is it not, that a man should always wash his hands before eating? Do you think, Jesus, that I am a bad man because I have to eat my lunch without washing my hands?"

"Certainly not," said Jesus with a smile. "You are not a bad man simply because you eat without washing your hands when you are in the fields and cannot do so. Unwashed hands cannot make a person bad anyway. Goodness and badness are inside of you, not in your skin." Then another man spoke up and asked another question.

"There are many of us here, Jesus, who have never learned to read. We have not gone to school. We have not been able to study the laws in the Bible. We can't remember all the laws the preachers in the synagogue tell us about. There seem to be hundreds of laws the preachers say we must follow if we want to please God. But we simply cannot remember them all. Do you think, Jesus, that we are bad because we can't remember all the laws? Our other teachers seem to think we are no good just because we don't know much." Then Jesus would encourage these people. He would say:

"For many years, our teachers have been adding more and more laws to the ones that are in the Bible. They have meant to help us but what they have really done is to make living a good life so hard that none of us can be counted good.

"I say to you, friends, that being good is not just obeying a large number of rules. You could obey every single one of the rules the teachers have made, and still not be really good. Whether one is good or not depends on how one feels inside in one's heart. Do you feel hateful or loving toward others? Do you feel angry or patient with the person who hurts you? Those are the things that count."

"That kind of talk sounds good, Jesus," said a man who had been busy all day long hauling stones for building a road. "But I wish you would tell us in just one sentence what is most important so that we can't forget." Jesus smiled at this and said:

"Your wish reminds me of what someone once said to Hillel, that great teacher of ours of whom you all have heard. The story is told of how a man one day said to Hillel: 'Tell me, Master, what all the laws put together mean and tell me so simply that I can hear it all while I stand on one foot.'" At this everyone laughed.

"Hillel gave the man a very good answer and a very short one," said Jesus. "Hillel said: *Never do to anyone else the kind of thing that is hateful to you.* This is all the laws put together. All the rest is just an explanation of that one short rule.'" Then Jesus added his own thought.

"I would say this rule in just a little different way. I would say it this way. *Do those things to others that you would like to have others do to you.*"

"That's a good rule," said the workman who had asked the question. "I could have stood on one foot easily while you said that."

"Try the rule," said Jesus. "It doesn't take long to say it, but it may take a long time to learn to follow it."

When his talk was over, the people got up from the ground and walked along the shore to their homes. Some of them seemed very much relieved. Jesus had given them something they could understand and something they could not forget.

"Do those things to others that you would like to have others do to you." It was a very short rule, but one that is still remembered after nearly two thousand years. We call it our Golden Rule.

> *Do those things to others that you would like to have others do to you.*

The Boy
Who Was Afraid
to Try

A Story from Uganda

ONCE UPON A TIME in a village in Africa there was a potter and his wife who had a son named Kumba. Now Kumba was a queer boy. The older he grew the queerer he became and the more his parents worried about him.

One trouble was that Kumba was small for his age. When he played with the other boys of the village he was not able to do as many things as they could. He was often beaten in games and his playmates teased him.

So Kumba began to play by himself. The more he kept away from the other boys the more afraid of them he grew and the more lonesome he felt. He wanted so badly to be somebody and yet he could not do the things that would make other boys notice him. Finally he became afraid even to try to do things lest someone might smile at his awkwardness. He would not even try to make bowls and vases out of clay as his father did. Kumba was afraid his father might

25

smile at these bowls and say they were poorly done. Kumba would not even try to learn to dig in the garden. So the boy spent most of his days wandering idly about in the fields and woods alone, dreaming and wishing all the time that he might some day be very wise and great, and yet he was afraid to learn how. The people of the village shook their heads and said: "Kumba must be stupid. His mind is of no account." The neighbor women came to comfort his mother:

"Don't feel so bad. Some day you will have another baby, and he will be like other children." But Kumba's mother said:

"I don't want any other baby. I want this boy of mine to be wise and good."

The men of the village came to encourage the father by saying: "Be patient. In time you will know whether your son is a stupid fool or whether he is really bright."

One day when Kumba was supposed to be asleep, he overheard his parents talking together about him. He was startled. He realized then that they were worried. They actually thought their boy might be a fool. Yet Kumba himself did not think he was stupid.

One evening in a gloomy mood, the boy wandered off into the woods alone. The sun was hanging low in the sky. He came to a hillside with a clearing beyond, from which he could watch the glowing clouds of evening. He sat down and covered his face with his hands, discouraged enough to cry.

Presently a Lion came quietly out of the woods. He saw Kumba and walked over toward him. "What are you doing here?" asked the Lion.

"I am feeling miserable," said Kumba. "I wish so much to be wise and great, but I don't know whether I am really bright or whether I am a fool."

"Is that all you are thinking about?" asked the Lion.

"Yes," said Kumba. "I think about it day and night."

"Then you *are* a fool," said the Lion. "Wise people think about what they can do for their country." The Lion turned about and ran back into the woods.

Presently an Antelope came leaping over the hillside. "What are you doing here?" asked the Antelope.

"I am feeling miserable," said Kumba. "I wish so much to be wise and great, but I do not know whether I am really bright or whether I am a fool."

"What do you eat?" asked the Antelope looking at the boy's thin legs.

"My mother cooks me two meals a day," said Kumba, "and I eat them."

"Do you ever thank your mother?"

"No, I don't remember."

"Well, you *are* a fool. All wise persons thank those who are kind to them," said the Antelope and off he leaped across the clearing.

Soon a Leopard came by and looked at Kumba suspiciously. "What are you doing here?" he asked.

"I am feeling miserable," said Kumba. "I wish so much to be wise and great, but I don't know whether I am bright or whether I am a fool."

"Do the other boys of the village like you?" asked the Leopard.

"No, I don't think they do. And I don't care. I don't like them either. They are mean to me."

"Then you *are* a fool. Don't you know that all boys are worth getting acquainted with, and that a wise person tries to do things *with* others?" The Leopard then darted off into the woods.

Soon an Elephant came shuffling along through the grass and looked down upon the boy. "What are you doing here?" asked the Elephant.

"I'm miserable," said Kumba. "I wish so much to be wise and great, but I do not know whether I am bright or whether I am a fool."

"What work do you do?" asked the Elephant.

"I don't do any work," said Kumba.

"Well, you *are* a fool!" said the Elephant. "All wise people work." And the Elephant turned around, made a disgusted twist of his tail, and ambled down the hillside.

By this time Kumba was ready to cry. Presently he heard a gentle little voice at his side. "What are you doing here?" asked a little grey Rabbit.

"Oh, I am feeling miserable. I wish so much to be wise, and all the animals have told me that I am a fool." For a moment the rabbit did not speak. He just let the boy cry.

Then the little grey Rabbit scampered up very close to Kumba, and whispered: "Which animals said you were a fool?"

"Well," said Kumba, "the Lion said I was a fool because I spend all my time thinking about myself. The Antelope said I was a fool because I have not been thanking my mother for the food she cooks for me. The Leopard said I was a fool because I don't play with the other boys. The Elephant said I was a fool because I don't do any work." The little grey Rabbit nodded her head.

"No wonder you feel like crying, for the animals have told you the truth. Wise people do not think about themselves all the time. Wise people do say 'thank you' when others do them favors. A wise boy does play with other children. And wise people work."

No words passed between Kumba and the little grey Rabbit for a long time. Little by little the darkness fell all around like a black mist. The little grey Rabbit invited Kumba to spend the night in the woods. He could lie down near the Rabbit's hole and be safe. So Kumba and the little grey Rabbit walked away together.

While Kumba lay on the grass in the dark he began to

think more courageously about himself until finally he fell asleep. By the time morning came Kumba decided that he *had been* a fool but he *was not going to be* a fool any longer.

Early in the morning he walked back to his home. When he first saw his mother he greeted her with a smile and a bright "Good morning!" When she later started out to dig yams in the field, Kumba found another hoe so that he could help. When the boys of the village began chasing one another, Kumba ran with them and didn't give up when he fell behind.

In the afternoon Kumba even sat down beside his father as he molded clay into bowls and asked if he might try his hand at the work. He knew his first bowl would be poorly made, but Kumba was no longer afraid to try to learn.

As the days passed and Kumba felt less and less afraid he began to ask questions. He asked his father how he made the dyes he used for painting his bowls. Kumba went to the fields with his father to gather the leaves and flowers which they later boiled to make the paints.

So the days and the weeks and the years went by. Kumba grew to be a man. By the time his father was an old man Kumba had become the famous potter of the village. People used to come from miles around to buy his bowls. They really were beautiful, too, and different from other bowls. Most of them were black with red or white designs painted on them.

And what meant more to Kumba even than the praise given him for his beautiful pottery was that his neighbors liked him. They no longer thought him a fool. His people called him wise and great.

The Bell
of
Atri

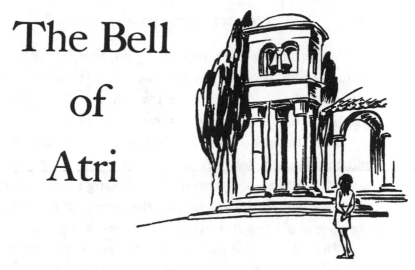

A Story from Sicily

THIS STORY HAPPENED long ago before there were any clocks or watches to tell time by. In those far-off days, the great big bells that hung high in the church steeples were really needed. For how could people without clocks or watches know when to come to church unless the bells in the steeples called them to come?

But the big bell in the town of Atri on a hillside in Sicily was not a church bell. The bell of Atri has a story all its own. It is about Good King John and his new idea for a town bell.

Without telling his people what he was going to do, Good King John had a tower built in the center of the large open market place where the farmers came weekday mornings to buy and sell their vegetables and fruits. From the roof of this tower the King had a large bell hung. To the bell he had a rope fastened that reached all the way to the ground so that anyone who wished could pull the rope and thus ring the bell.

While all this work was going on, the people were very curious to know what the bell was for. Finally, when the tower was finished and the bell was hung, Good King John was ready to tell the people about his new idea.

He mounted his royal white horse. With footmen going before, blowing their trumpets, and with riders following behind to make a big procession, the King rode up and down and back and forth through all the streets of the town, calling the people to gather in the open market place.

When the people inside their houses heard the trumpets blowing, and when they looked out their doors and saw their Good King John riding on his beautiful white horse, they rushed from their homes. In a short while the market square was crowded with men and women and children all talking at once and making a big noise.

Presently the trumpeters blew three loud blasts one after the other, and everyone became quiet. Then in a loud clear voice, Good King John spoke:

"Men and women of Atri, the bell hanging in this market place I have had put here for you. Any one of you may come and ring it, old or young, rich or poor. But no one must ring it unless he has been unfairly treated by someone else. This is a Bell of Justice.

"I have appointed a man among you to be your Judge. Whenever in the day or night he hears this bell ringing, he shall come at once to the market place to talk with the bell ringer. You and he will then plan for a meeting in his home. Everyone who has had any part in the wrongdoing will be told to come, and all those who saw what happened should also come. When you have all gathered, and you have told the Judge the whole story, he will decide what should be done. Perhaps he can help you make the wrong right. Perhaps he will show you what you can do to prevent the same kind of wrong being done again. Perhaps he will decide on a punishment for the wrongdoer, so that he will remember.

"Let this bell in Atri, then, be called a Bell of Justice. I want you, my people of Atri, to live together in happiness. In order to do so, each one must feel that he is always being treated justly."

When the people of Atri heard Good King John's words they were very much pleased and cheered loudly.

After that the little town of Atri was different. Some ran often to the Bell to give it a ring. Others were more timid in making their grudges known and in showing their hurt feelings. Even children sometimes rang the Bell. At first it was exciting to ring it, but then the meeting with the Judge afterwards was not always so much fun.

The Judge listened patiently to everyone. He always helped the one who thought himself wronged to tell his whole story. But he was also very fair to the one who was blamed. He was not easily fooled when someone tried to cover up the truth.

As the days and the months passed many a quarrel was stopped in its beginning. Often the very thought of the Bell kept quarrels from starting. Even parents began trying harder to be fair to all their children. Playmates began treating one another with more kindness. After a long, long while, there came a time when the Bell was almost never rung. Good King John was much pleased.

Year after year went by. The rope that hung from the Bell began to wear out and to ravel at the end. Strand after strand loosened. Little by little the loose strands rotted and broke off. Finally the end of the rope was so high that no one but a very tall man could reach it. At last someone decided to mend the rope. This he did by tying some branches of grapevines to its lower end. In doing this, he left the leaves and tendrils on the branches.

Now in the castle on the hillside above the town there had long lived a Knight. When he was young he had been very fond of hunting. Riding forth on his favorite horse, armed with his bow and arrows, he used to hunt in the forest for wild boar and deer. Many a feast he had given in his banquet hall where he had served delicious roast pig and wild fowl shot down by his own arrows.

Now that the Knight was too old to hunt he had lost all interest in that sport, and no longer even cared for his horses or his hunting dogs. So he sold all his fine horses except the one that had been his particular favorite. He also sold all his dogs, and even his gardens and his vineyards. The more money he got, the more he wanted. All day long he would sit in his chair thinking only of himself, and counting out his money.

As time went on, this old Knight decided it was a waste to feed even his favorite old horse, since he was no longer of any use. So the Knight ordered that the horse be untied and put out of his stall and left to wander uncared for over the hillsides. The old horse became as the wild animals of the woods, obliged to hunt his own food and water. Yet unafraid, he wandered up and down the streets of the town.

The townspeople often felt sorry for the horse as they watched him drag his old legs along through the streets and lanes, hunting for garbage, or drinking some water at the village fountain. Often the dogs fought with him over scraps of food, and the thorns and rocks on the hillsides where he lay down to rest made sores on his old body.

One hot summer day, while the people of Atri were taking their afternoon naps in their quiet homes, they were suddenly awakened by the ringing of the town Bell. The startled Judge turned on his couch and listened. He rose, put on his clothes and hurried to the market place. All the while the Bell kept ringing the old song: "Someone has done a wrong! Someone has done a wrong!" And all the while the Judge kept wondering: "Who can it be?"

As he entered the corner of the market place, to his surprise he saw, standing under the Bell in the tower, not

a man, not a woman, not even a child, but a poor old horse! He was tugging away and chewing the dry leaves that had been fastened to the rope! As the Judge came closer he recognized the Knight's favorite old horse. "Well, well," said the Judge to himself, "this poor dumb old horse is doing more than he knows. He is asking for justice."

In the meantime the whole town had been awakened. Soon a noisy crowd was gathering in the market place. Each one had his own story to tell of the cruel ways in which the old horse had been treated. The Judge called the old Knight to come before him to hear what the people were saying.

At first the old Knight merely laughed at them all as if the whole affair were a joke. But the Judge said solemnly that it was no laughing matter. Here was a dumb animal unable to plead his own cause, who had for many years given his master faithful and excellent service. And now in his old age he had been thrown out of his barn, and left without food or shelter from the rain or sun or cold.

"I command you, Sir Knight, from this time on to give this old horse good food and the shelter of a clean stall, and to give him also the freedom of your own grassy fields."

On hearing the Judge's words, the old Knight hung his head in shame, but he promised to do as the Judge had commanded. The cheering crowd formed a marching line and led the old horse home to his stall as if they were leading a king to his throne.

When Good King John heard the story, he laughed and laughed. "Right well I'm pleased," he said. "Church bells at best call people to church, but my Bell of Atri does more. Even the dumb animals can use it to call for justice. The Bell of Atri shall be long remembered."

The King Who Changed His Mind

A Story from India

LONG, LONG AGO in India lived Prince Asoka. From the time he was a small child his mother had told him stories about his grandfather—the first great King of India. She would say:

"Your grandfather was a very great man, my son. He made our India the greatest country in all the world. His armies conquered one small country after another until our kingdom now stretches from ocean to ocean. Some day, my son, you will become the King of this great land."

Then the young Prince would sit up straight in his chair and feel very proud. He would wonder. "If I am the King of the greatest country in all the world, will I be the greatest King in all the world?" His mother would then smile and say:

"You talk like a child, my son. You do not yet know how hard it is to be a great King over a big country. Our enemies are all around us. You will have to be prepared to fight at any time. There is still one country over by the sea, that has never given up fighting us. These Kalingas are fierce soldiers. They can shoot their arrows straight and far. We are not safe until these people also are conquered and their arrows and bows and horses and chariots are taken from them. Asoka, my son, this is the first thing you must do when you become King. You must fight the Kalingas!"

Over and over the Prince's mother had said these things to her son. And every day he was reminded that he must learn how to fight. Every day he saw soldiers with swords in their belts marching about the palace gardens. Every day he saw them practice shooting with arrows and bows. Soon Prince Asoka was given his own small sword and soon he was practicing with his own small arrows and bow. Every day the young Prince watched his father drive about the palace gardens in his royal chariot. Soon Prince Asoka was allowed to stand beside his father in the chariot and to practice shooting his arrows as the horses ran.

All these happenings took place in the great big palace grounds. All around these grounds was a high wall. Outside the high wall was the big city. Outside the big city were the forests where the wild deer leaped and the elephants tramped and the peacocks strutted.

But Prince Asoka was a big boy before he was allowed to go outside the wall into the big city streets. And he was a tall young man before he was allowed to hunt the wild deer and the peacocks in the forest.

Even then the Prince was never allowed to go outside the palace grounds alone. He would always ride forth on the back of one of the royal white elephants, while soldiers with spears in their hands ran alongside. Other soldiers would line the streets on both sides as he rode through the big city.

Nor were strangers allowed inside the palace wall without being carefully examined. It is said that anyone unknown to the guards was stripped of his clothes and made to bathe. The orders were that the guards must make sure that no one entering the garden carried under his clothes a hidden knife or a bottle of poison. The rumor was that at mealtimes, every bowl of food brought to the King's table was first tasted by some faithful servant to make sure that it had not been secretly poisoned.

In these many ways Asoka and his family were carefully guarded day and night, because they were always afraid that someone might secretly do them harm.

But why should the King of the great land of India be so afraid? Did he not have a larger army and more horses and chariots and money than anyone else? Prince Asoka never stopped to ask such questions. He simply took these things for granted as a natural part of being a Prince.

So it was that when Prince Asoka was crowned King, he had one big ambition and that was to be a fighting King like his grandfather before him. He began at once to do as his mother had told him. He started to plan how to fight the Kalingas. Soon thousands of well-armed soldiers marched off to make the attack and King Asoka commanded them to fight hard and fast.

It was not long, therefore, until the victorious armies came marching home. On foot, on horseback, on elephants and in chariots they paraded through the streets of the big city. Behind them walked a long procession of frightened men, women and children from the land of Kalinga. With drooping heads, and with hands tied behind their backs they came. Miserable captives soon to be sold like sheep, and led off to strange houses, to work for strange men.

With great pride King Asoka watched the long parade. Now, at last he had proved that he was a strong King like his grandfather. Beyond all doubt his kingdom was now the greatest in the world.

But something soon happened that King Asoka had not counted on. One day there chanced to come into the palace gardens a young Beggar dressed in a yellow robe, carrying an empty bowl. He asked for rice. The guards searched him from head to foot and finally let him in. The young man's manner was gentle, and goodness seemed to shine in his eyes. King Asoka liked him the moment he first caught sight of him. The young man was allowed to stay in the palace gardens.

Before long the King and the Beggar became friends. They would sit together in the garden for long hours at a time and talk. The King had never met a person like him before. All the show and pomp of the palace had no glory for the visiting Beggar. He took no interest in the delicious foods served on the King's table. All the young man asked for was a quiet place in the grass where he might sleep, and a bowl filled with rice twice a day. When talking with the King, the young man never flattered or praised him for his successful war against the Kalingas. Instead, before long he began to talk of the foolishness of fighting. He said:

"I am a follower of the great Buddha. He used to say: 'What do we gain by our fighting and killing? What do we gain by our overeating and by our overdrinking? What do we gain by living just for our own pleasure? Some day we shall all die and there will be nothing worth remembering about us.' You, O King, have conquered the Kalingas, and yet you are afraid of them. What would you gain, even if you conquered the whole world, if the people you conquered hated you? King Asoka, the truth is that the Kalingas would like to kill you and forget you ever lived." King Asoka listened but did not understand. He asked:

"What did Buddha mean by his words?" Patiently the young man explained more fully.

"The things that last, O King, are gained through gentleness and kindness. You can never really conquer people by fighting them. If you are cruel to others, they in turn will wish to be cruel to you. And you will live always in fear of what harm they may do to you. On the other hand, if you feel generous and kind toward others, kind feelings will slowly grow in them also. They will become your friends. You will have no one to be afraid of."

"But a King has to show his people that he is strong, doesn't he? His soldiers must keep the people afraid."

"Not so, O King," answered the young man. "Think no more about your own power and strength. Think rather about your people; how you can make their lives happier. See that the sick are cared for. Feed those who are hungry. Instead of carefully guarding all your treasures behind these walls, give away your money to those who have not enough. Instead of sending soldiers out to kill, send men out to all parts of your kingdom to teach the people how to improve their ways of living."

Week after week the young man stayed within the palace grounds. Day after day he and the King talked together. Sometimes King Asoka felt very uncomfortable with the young man's new thoughts. "Shouldn't I have fought the people of Kalinga? Has it all been a mistake? Wasn't my grandfather a great King after all?"

The longer King Asoka thought on these matters, the more he began to wonder how the people of Kalinga must have felt when his soldiers marched into their towns. Many thousands of the Kalingas had been killed in that short war! And every single one of those thousands was somebody's brother or son, or mother or child. Other thousands had been hurt. They had lost arms, legs, eyes or hands. Homes had been burned, children had been left without fathers, women without husbands. Thousands of others had been stolen from their homes, and even then they were working for strangers hundreds of miles away from their homes. Was it his fault that all these people were lonely and heartbroken? Was he responsible for the thousands who had been killed?

Such thoughts were frightening. King Asoka sometimes screamed at night in his dreams. In the daytime he began to lose interest in dancing and feasting and hunting. He began to hate the very sight of soldiers with spears and arrows. What ought he to do? For a long time King Asoka was undecided, but when he once made up his mind, he was no longer afraid of what anyone might say or do. He was no longer afraid of being killed. He knew he had found something to live for that dying could not destroy. He was like a new man. His gentle friend with the bowl of rice was happy beyond words. And what was it King Asoka had decided on?

First of all, he sent hundreds of messengers from one end of his kingdom to the other. He said:

"Tell my people that I have changed my mind. I am through with all wars and all fighting!" He even sent messengers to the Kalingas to tell them that he was sorry for all the sadness he had brought them by his fighting. He said:

"Pass my words along to all the people. Say to them: 'You are all my children, and, just as I wish happiness for the children in my own home, so I wish happiness to every one of you.'

"I want everyone to know also that I have arranged that if a dispute arises among you anywhere which I could help to settle, my officers are to call me no matter what hour of the day or night it may be. It does not matter whether I am dining or am in bed or out in my chariot, or in the palace gardens, I want to help you."

King Asoka, however, did much more than talk and have his messengers pass on his instructions. He began at once to see that things were done. He had deep wells dug near villages where people had been drinking from the muddy waters of pools. He had shade trees and fruit trees planted along the roadsides, and rest houses built for travelers. He had small hospitals put up where the sick could be cared for. He had the people instructed in the use of plants as medicines for animals as well as for people, and he gave away seeds for planting.

One day a man was brought before the King. He was accused of having stolen a bag of rice. The King asked: "Did you steal the bag of rice?" The thief answered: "Yes."

"Why did you steal?"

"Because, O King, I had no way of making my living and I and my children were starving." Then King Asoka blushed, for he felt ashamed.

"If there is anyone among my people who is hungry, it is I who have made him hungry," he said. "If there is anyone who is cold, it is I who have made him cold." He then commanded that a box of jewels be brought and opened.

"Choose whichever piece you wish. Take it, sell it and buy food," said the King to the thief. The man was so surprised that he hesitated and bowed low before the King before he even touched one of the jewels.

King Asoka began to treat his people in many such generous ways. Before long they stopped quarreling and stealing. Those who had more than the rest began to divide what

they had with those who had less. Swords and spears rusted in the storerooms. The prisons were soon almost empty.

As for himself and his royal family, King Asoka announced that the law of kindness would apply to animals as well as to people. Formerly many deer and peacocks had been shot daily and cooked in the royal kitchens, but now the King would no longer eat the meat of birds or animals of any kind.

He wanted to make sure that his people would never forget the way of kindness. He wanted to make sure also that his sons and his grandsons and his great grandsons, who would some day be Kings in his place, would never forget. So this is what King Asoka did.

He commanded his men to quarry large stones out of the ground and to set them up at many different places by the roadside. He wrote out the words to be carved deep into these stones, that passers-by could read. Some stones he had cut into the shape of high pillars. These he had set up in front of the temples, and his words were carved deep into these pillars. These were the words:

"The only lasting pleasure will be found in patience and gentleness. The only true conquest is that which is brought about by kindness. I have written these words that my sons and grandsons, and all those who come after me may never forget. Let this Law of Life be remembered as long as there is a sun and moon in the sky."

If, some day, you should be traveling in the land of India perhaps you will ask where one of these old stone monuments still stands. Then you may go and see for yourself the words that King Asoka had carved into stone more than two thousand years ago.

The Naumburg Children's Festival

A Story from Germany

LONG AGO BEFORE there were airplanes or bombs or even before there were any guns with which to shoot, men fought each other with bows and arrows, spiked clubs, or with swords and spears. In that long ago time, the people of Bohemia and the people of Germany were at war with each other.

The men of Bohemia were big and strong. For twelve long years their general, Procop,[1] had been leading the armies up and down the hills of Germany, burning town after town and killing many people. They had killed so many people that all over Germany the very name of Procop was hated.

One afternoon in June the watchman on the tower of the wall around the town of Naumburg looked across the Saale river flowing along not far from the wall, and saw coming down the hillside a long line of war wagons, and

---

[1] Procop lived in Bohemia in the fifteenth century A.D.

beyond the war wagons the dark moving forms of thousands of warriors. He saw the flashing of their shields in the sunlight and the glint of their long spears above their heads. Faintly he heard shouting and singing.

When the watchman told the people of the town what he had seen, all the men, women and children of Naumburg were frightened beyond words. Messengers ran hurriedly to the fields, calling the farmers in from plowing in their gardens, and the shepherds in from watching their sheep on the hillsides.

When all were safely inside the city wall, the big iron gate was locked. For one long month no one went in or out of the gate.

The gardens in the fields outside were full of ripening vegetables but no one in Naumburg could gather them. Along the roadside were many cherry trees, and the cherries were ripening, but no one in Naumburg could pick the cherries.

Each day there was less and less food stored away in the barns and cupboards of the town. Soon there would be no flour with which to bake bread. Soon the housewives would have no meat or vegetables to boil in the pot on the stove.

The Lord of the Castle on the hill walked back and forth in his garden, cursing Procop and his army. The peasant farmers sat idly in the streets. Mothers talked with one another of their hungry children. The children were almost afraid to play.

But this was not all. Everyone in the town was dreaming of something worse that was still to come.

Each morning they heard the rumble of the big war wagons of Procop as they were driven around and around the walls outside the town, and the furious singing of the soldiers frightened them.

All the while the great army of Procop was camping on the hillside on the opposite side of the Saale River. While the Naumburg people were starving, the Bohemian soldiers were enjoying the German vegetable gardens, tramping and burning their wheat and barley fields, and feasting on the luscious cherries ripening on the cherry trees.

But the helpless and starving people of Naumburg were determined not to give up, and Procop, after waiting one whole month, lost his temper. So one morning, after his war wagons had taken their daily journey around the town wall, and his men had once more sung their furious war songs, Procop put on his broad-brimmed black hat and his long black coat and high-heeled boots, and rode on his horse across the bridge and up to the great iron gate. With all his might he threw a big paper roll over the wall.

In great excitement, the Naumburg soldiers ran with the roll and gave it to the Lord of the Castle. Unrolling it he read these words:

"If Naumburg does not surrender to General Procop and his army before the end of this week, he will enter the town and kill every man, woman and child within the walls."

Below was the General's name.

News of the message spread like fire through the town. The Lord of the Castle called a meeting of all the men to decide what should be done. A sad company it was that gathered together. They could scarcely find words with which to tell one another their thoughts. To give up or to die, which was worse? They could see no way of escape.

The next day the men again gathered in the town hall and the Lord of the Castle sat before them in his big chair. One after another the rich and important men of the town spoke.

"There is nothing to do but give up," they said.

"We dare not fight this army of giants. Death by the sword or death from hunger is all that awaits us if we hold on." Yet they could not agree to give up. All were in despair.

Finally, the schoolmaster arose, and bowing very low so that his braided hair stood out behind like a horn, he said:

"My Lord, may I be permitted to speak?"

"Speak," said the Lord of the Castle.

"Procop is very fat," said the schoolmaster.

"His fatness will not make us any fatter," interrupted one of the men.

"Fat men are very wise," said the teacher.

"All the worse for us, if we fall into the hands of a wise man," said another.

"But wise, fat men love children," said the teacher, pointing his finger at the men in the hall.

"Procop may love his own children, but he does not love our children," said one of the men.

"Listen to me," said the teacher. "Procop does love children and when they are around him he becomes jolly. He does not look so tall when he bends over and romps and plays with them. This is my plan. Call the children together—all those between seven and fourteen. Tell them we will open the big iron gate if they will go together in a procession across the river, singing all the way to the camp of Procop. Tell them to curtsy their prettiest and to ask Procop to play with them. As he plays with them his hard heart will grow kind again. Tell the children to ask Procop then for their sakes to save the town of Naumburg."

It was a very strange suggestion. Would the children do it? After all the stories they had heard of the cruel Procop, would they have the courage to face him and ask him to play with them? If his heart did not soften, the children would be the first to die. It seemed cruel to ask such a thing of the children, yet no one could think of anything else.

Finally, all the children of the town were called together and the teacher told them the plan. Some of the children cried. Some said: "We cannot, we are afraid." Others said: "Yes, we will do it, whether we are afraid or not."

Early the next morning, the mothers of Naumburg washed their children's faces and hands and brushed their hair and put on their prettiest dresses and suits. Then what did the soldiers of Procop see? The great iron gate swung open and a long procession of singing children tripped happily over the bridge, across the Saale River and up the hillside toward the camp of their enemies. The surprised soldiers could do nothing but stare at the children.

Standing before his tent door, the tall fat General was watching them. He stood straight and stern. His eyes grew big. Then over his lips there spread a wee smile. The children's singing and skipping reminded him of his own children and a big tear rolled down one fat cheek. When he saw the children turn to come up the hill to his very own tent, he could wait no longer. He walked out to meet them.

The boys touched their hats and the girls curtsied their prettiest. "Good Procop, we have come to play with you," they cried.

His smile grew bigger. He sat down under a big cherry tree. The girls climbed up on his lap. The boys began playing with his funny fat legs. They played roly-poly in the grass. The mothers and fathers behind the stone walls of Naumburg heard the children laughing. Finally, the big fat General called out to his men:

"It is no use. I cannot bear to see these brave children suffer. This time I am the one who will have to surrender. Bring me a large basket of cherries." The children all sat down in the grass around Procop and they had a cherry feast.

Late in the afternoon, as they parted, the children hugged and kissed the big General and said in their sweetest voices:

"We thank you that for our sakes you are going to spare Naumburg."

That night the moon rose and spread its silver light over the quiet waters of the Saale River. A rumbling of wagon wheels broke the stillness, and a long line of black shadows moved up the hillside and out over the fields beyond, away from the town of Naumburg.

When the morning sun rose in the sky, the watchman looked down from his tower toward the enemy's camp. Procop and his army were gone. Never a happier day began than that 28th day of July, over five hundred years ago.

For many years the town of Naumburg has been celebrating this 28th day of July with a *kinderfest,* which means a "children's feast." Sometimes they call it "The Cherry Feast of Naumburg." It is all in honor of those brave children who played with the General.

The Richest
King in
the World

A Story from Greece

LONG, LONG AGO there lived a King named Croesus,[1] who was thought to be the richest King in all the world.

One day a visitor named Solon from the country of Greece came to see this famous King. Solon was the ruler of the important city of Athens, and was famous for his wisdom. But he had always lived in a plain house and he always wore simple clothes.

When Solon first met the royal guards at the gate and was ushered up the steps into the great reception hall of the rich King's palace, he realized that here was everything that money could buy.

On entering the great throne room, Solon walked down the long hall between two rows of stately pillars toward the King's high throne. After kneeling and saying all the polite words one is expected to say to kings, Solon had a good chance to look at Croesus and to see the splendor of his

[1] Pronounced Kréesus.

robes. A gown of royal purple covered him from head to foot. On his head gleamed a golden crown set with sapphires, rubies and diamonds. Sparkling beads hung about his neck. Holding out his scepter as a welcome to his famous visitor, King Croesus smiled on Solon and altogether looked very grand and pleased that this famous wise man from Greece had come to visit him.

After questioning his famous visitor about the comforts of his voyage across the ocean from Greece, King Croesus suggested that they take a walk together about the palace. So he stepped down from his throne and took Solon personally through room after room. King Croesus proudly pointed out a beautiful rug from India in one room, a bed and chairs from Egypt in another, and beautifully woven couch covers and cushions from Persia. The King had big chests of drawers opened, and had spread out before Solon's eyes hundreds of silk and linen garments of the most delicate colors and designs.

Servants went to the royal storerooms and brought out rare bowls and plates and vases of silver and gold, also statues carved in wood and stone. Altogether King Croesus showed his famous visitor hundreds of beautiful things that merchants had brought to him from many different countries of the world. Finally, the King said to his visiting friend:

"Wise Solon, have you ever seen more beautiful things than these that I have been showing you?"

"Your Majesty," said Solon quietly, "these things you have shown me are indeed beautiful but they are not the most beautiful things I have ever seen." King Croesus was more than surprised, but he tried to be polite.

"What could you have seen more beautiful?" he asked.

"Your Majesty, I once saw a peacock, and it glittered more brilliantly than any of the colors your most skilled weavers have been able to put into your garments. I have seen also a wild pheasant in the woods. I consider it more beautiful than anything here. Nothing that men can make can compare in beauty to the feathers of these living birds."

King Croesus was annoyed, but he said nothing. He had never before met a man so blunt and outspoken.

In the evening the rich man and the wise man were dining together. The King, having drunk freely of his wine, was in the jolliest of moods and even more sure of himself than before. He smiled proudly at his visitor and said:

"Tell me now, O Solon, who do you think is the happiest man you have ever seen?" He expected, of course, that Solon would say: "I have never seen anyone happier than you, O King." But the wise Solon was quiet for a moment. He then said thoughtfully:

"I am thinking of a poor farmer who once lived in a small cottage in Athens. His name was Tellus. I think he was the happiest man I ever knew." Again King Croesus was more than surprised.

"How could a poor man like that be happier than a king such as I am?"

Solon continued without raising his voice.

"Your Majesty, Tellus had a wife and three children. He loved them all and they loved him. They had enough to eat, and enough money to supply their simple wants. His children were all well educated and they in turn had happy families of their own. Finally, when Greece needed soldiers, Tellus joined the army. He was killed in battle, but he was prepared to die, and his wife and children are still proud of him. His neighbors have never stopped talking of the many kind and good things that Tellus did for them." King Croesus disliked these remarks even more than what Solon had first said.

"So you think my happiness is as nothing compared with that of such a man?" he said in disgust.

"A poor man is often happier than a rich man," said Solon calmly. "I think also of two brothers whom I regard as happier than you. These two young men lived with their old mother. She had set her heart on attending a certain festival in the temple in the big city of Athens. But when the day came for her to go, the oxen that were to pull the cart in which she was to ride were being used in plowing a distant field and could not be brought back in time. What could the two sons do? They were determined that their good old mother should not be disappointed. They puzzled over the matter a long time. Finally they thought of a plan, but they imagined everybody would laugh at them if they followed it. Yet they decided they preferred to be made fun of rather than to disappoint their good old mother.

"So what did they do? They hitched themselves to the cart as if they were oxen and these two sons pulled their good old mother all the way to the temple in Athens.

"Instead of making fun of the two men, the people who saw them cheered and praised them. At the festival they were welcomed with honor, and all three joined merrily in the whole celebration. I believe they were two of the happiest men I have ever known." By this time King Croesus had lost his patience.

"Why is it that you make me of no account? How can

you place these poor working people above the richest king in the world?"

"O King, I must speak plainly. You should know that it is not possible yet to tell how truly happy you are. No one knows how long all these treasures will be yours. Suppose you should lose them all. Suppose you should be deprived of your kingdom and should be made a prisoner. Would you still be happy? No, O King, I cannot tell how truly happy you really are until I know how you will behave when you come to die."

With these words, the conversation between King Croesus and Solon ended. The next morning the visitor left for his home.

Many years passed by. In another country there arose another powerful king whose name was Cyrus. King Cyrus gathered large armies and with them marched from one country to another. He conquered wherever he went until his great kingdom was the largest in the world.

King Cyrus marched against King Croesus. Although Croesus fought stubbornly, the enemy entered his capital city, carried away all his precious treasures, burned his palace and finally made Croesus a prisoner. When all was over King Cyrus said:

"King Croesus has been a very stubborn enemy. Take him and make him an example to all littler kings who may think they can fight me successfully."

The soldiers of the mighty Cyrus obeyed. They dragged Croesus to the market place. There they made a big pile of dry sticks and logs. They tied the poor King to a stake in the middle of the pile. Then one of the men ran to get a lighted torch in order to set the King and the pile on fire.

As poor Croesus stood helplessly with hands and feet tied, thinking he would soon be burned alive, he remembered the words that Solon had said to him years before: "No man can say whether or not you are really happy until he knows how you behave when you die." Croesus moaned in his agony: "O Solon! O Solon! O Solon!"

Now it so happened that King Cyrus was riding by at that very moment and heard the moaning of the man about to die.

"What does he say?" asked King Cyrus.

"Strange as it may seem," said one of King Cyrus' servants, "Croesus is calling the name of Solon, the old wise man of Greece." King Cyrus was curious. He rode up nearer the doomed man.

"Why do you call on the name of Solon?" he asked.

Croesus did not want to tell. He was quiet. King Cyrus repeated his question. Finally Croesus had to tell the whole story of Solon's visit to his palace many years before. King Cyrus was touched. He wondered what his own end might be, and he had pity on Croesus.

"Untie the ropes! Let Croesus go free!" he commanded. It is said that after that, as long as Croesus lived, King Cyrus treated his old enemy as a friend.

The Wind
and the Sun

A Story from Greece

THE WIND AND THE SUN were arguing with each
other.

"I am stronger than you are," boasted the Wind to
the Sun.

"No! I am stronger than you are," the Sun declared
very emphatically.

While the two were thus contradicting each other, they
looked down on the earth and saw a man walking along a
road. The sight of this man gave the Sun an idea.

"Let us make an experiment," he said. "Let us see which
one of us can make that man take off his cloak. The one
who succeeds will plainly be the stronger."

The Wind remembered how many, many times he had
torn down big houses and blown down trees twice as high as
the man on the road. He said to himself:

"Surely I can soon tear a cloak off a man's back." So the
Wind gave his consent to the experiment.

"Very well, you try first," said the Sun. So he hid behind a cloud and waited, trying to peep through a tiny crack to watch the Wind.

Then the Wind began. At first he blew only moderately fast, then harder and more furiously. He pounded and he slapped and he whirled and he jerked. But the louder he roared, and the faster he blew, the more closely the traveler wrapped his cloak around him. Finally, angry at the traveler and peeved with himself, the Wind had to give up.

Then the Sun came out from behind the cloud and began in all his glory to shine down on the traveler. The Sun did not move or make a sound. Its warm sunbeams reached quietly down and around until they touched with their warmth everything below. Soon the traveler began to feel warm. He opened up his cloak in order to feel cooler. Before long he was so hot he flung his cloak off entirely and carried it on his arm.

"Ha," said the Sun, "it seems to me that our argument is settled. You could not make that traveler take off his cloak, but I have not only made him take it off, I have even made him *keep* it off."

The Wind could find no words with which to answer the Sun, so he went off in his usual blustery way and did not argue any more.

The strength of the Wind is like the strength of a strong giant who overcomes others only by hurting them.

The strength of the Sun is like the strength of Love that warms the heart.

The Persevering Ant

A Story from the Indians of Brazil

Long, long ago when the earth was young, a little Ant went out into a snowy field. But she found she could not crawl, for the Snow held her feet fast.

"Snow, you are very strong," the Ant said. "You hold my feet so fast I cannot move. You must be the strongest thing in all the world."

"I am strong," said the Snow, "but I am not the strongest thing in all the world. The Sun above is stronger than I, for it simply shines down on me and I melt away and can do nothing about it."

So the Ant went up to the Sun and said:

"Sun, you are very strong, for you can melt away the Snow that holds my feet fast. You must be the strongest thing in all the world." The Sun said:

"I am strong, little Ant, but I am not the strongest thing in all the world for a Cloud can come along and cover my face and I can do nothing about it."

So the Ant went to the Cloud and said:

"O Cloud, you are very strong for you can cover the face of the Sun, that can melt the Snow, that can hold my feet fast. You must certainly be the strongest thing in all the world."

"I am strong, little Ant," said the Cloud, "but I am not the strongest thing in all the world, for the Wind may come along and blow me away, and I can do nothing about it."

So the Ant went to the Wind and said:

"O Wind, you are very strong. You can blow away the Cloud, that can hide the Sun, that can melt the Snow, that can hold my feet fast. You, Wind, must be the strongest thing in all the world."

"I am strong, little Ant," said the Wind, "but I am not the strongest thing in all the world, for a Wall can break me, and I cannot get by."

So the Ant went to the Wall and said:

"Wall, you are very strong. You can break the Wind, that can blow away the Cloud, that can hide the Sun, that can melt the Snow, that can hold my feet fast. You must be the strongest thing in all the world."

"I am strong, little Ant," said the Wall, "but I am not the strongest thing in all the world, for the Rat can gnaw a hole right through me and I can do nothing about it."

So the Ant went to the Rat and said:

"O Rat, you are very strong, for you can gnaw a hole through the Wall, that can break the Wind, that can blow away the Cloud, that can hide the Sun, that can melt the

Snow, that can hold my feet fast. You must be the strongest thing in all the world."

"I am strong, little Ant," said the Rat, "but I am not the strongest thing in all the world, for the Cat can catch me and eat me up, and I can do nothing about it."

So the Ant went to the Cat and said:

"O Cat, you are very strong for you can catch the Rat, that can gnaw a hole in the Wall, that can break the Wind, that can blow away the Cloud, that can hide the Sun, that can melt the Snow, that can hold my feet fast. You must be the strongest thing in all the world."

"I am strong, little Ant," said the Cat, "but I am not the strongest thing in all the world, for there is the Tiger that can catch me and eat me up, and I can do nothing about it."

So the Ant went to the Tiger and said:

"O Tiger, you are very strong, for you can kill the Cat, that can kill the Rat, that can gnaw a hole in the Wall, that can break the Wind, that can blow away the Cloud, that can hide the Sun, that can melt the Snow, that can hold my feet fast. You must be the strongest thing in all the world."

"I am strong, little Ant," said the Tiger, "but I am not the strongest thing in all the world, for there is Man who can shoot me with his arrow and kill me, and I can do nothing about it."

So the Ant went to Man and said:

"Man, you are very strong, for you can shoot and kill the Tiger, that can kill the Cat, that can kill the Rat, that can gnaw a hole in the Wall, that can break the Wind, that can blow away the Cloud, that can hide the Sun, that can melt the Snow, that can hold my feet fast. You, Man, must be the strongest thing in all the world."

"I am very strong, little Ant," said Man, "but I am not the strongest thing in all the world, for God made me."

So the Ant went to God and said:

"O God, you must be the strongest thing in all the world, for you made Man, that can shoot the Tiger, that can kill the Cat, that can catch the Rat, that can gnaw a hole in the Wall, that can break the Wind, that can blow away the Cloud, that can hide the Sun, that can melt the Snow, that can hold my feet fast."

And God said:

"Yes, little Ant, I am the strongest of all things. You are a very persevering little Ant to keep on asking and wondering who is the strongest until you came at last to Me."

Gautama Finds Out for Himself

A Story from India

PRINCE GAUTAMA LIVED in a palace in India a very long time ago. The grounds around the palace were like a large and beautiful park completely surrounded by a high wall. Servants, nurses, cooks, gardeners and helpers of all kinds were there to do things for the Prince.

Gautama was taught by special teachers who came to the palace just to teach him. He learned to read and to say verses from his bible. He was taught how to be a good son to his parents, and how to behave toward guests. He was taught also how to fight with a sword, how to ride a horse, and how to shoot with bow and arrows.

While Gautama was still a young child, a wise man had come to the King and predicted that something was going to happen to keep his son from ever becoming a king. The father was frightened and determined from that time on to protect his son from every possible harm. He made a strict rule that the Prince should never be allowed to go alone outside the palace grounds. He must not be permitted to see any sick person, or anyone blind or crippled or very old. And if anyone died, that person's death was not even mentioned where the Prince might hear. Everything ugly or frightening was to be kept out of his royal sight.

Merchants came to the palace to sell fruits, gold and silver ornaments, rugs and silks. Gautama hung around them asking questions about the lands from which they had come. In this way he learned of China and Arabia and Persia and Egypt and of the great ocean and of the ships that sailed across it. Naturally, Gautama began to wish that he, too, might travel about the world, and he began to fret over his father's rule that he must not go outside the palace grounds alone.

The King tried very hard to keep his son happy by giving him everything he could think of to enjoy. He chose the most beautiful young woman in all his kingdom to be his son's wife. The wedding was celebrated with the coming of many guests and with feasting and dancing. The King built three palaces just for the new bride and groom, one for winter, one for spring, and one for summer. Gautama and his wife seemed very happy. A little son was born and Gautama loved him dearly.

The sport that Gautama liked best was hunting. For this he was allowed to go outside the palace walls provided someone went along to protect him. He often rode out into the woods with his servant, Channa, to hunt for deer.

One day as they were riding along on their two horses, they came upon a man lying beside a rock, groaning and twitching in pain.

"What is wrong with this man?" asked Gautama.

"He is sick," said Channa.

"But why is he sick?" asked Gautama. "Can't we do anything to take away his pain?"

"It is the way of life," said Channa.

"But why should a man have to suffer so much pain?"

"This man is only a beggar, let us forget him," said Channa. But Gautama could not forget. He rode back to his palace and called his teachers and asked them:

"Why do men become sick?"

The teachers opened their bibles and read prayers for Gautama to repeat so that he would not be sick. But Gautama was not satisfied.

Again on another day he and his servant, Channa, were out hunting in the country. Gautama was full of life and well contented with himself. But as they rode along they met a man leaning heavily on two canes, scarcely able to push himself along. His hair was white, his face wrinkled and brown, and his hands shook like leaves in the wind.

"What is wrong with this man?" asked Gautama.

"He is old," answered Channa.

"What do you mean by 'old'?" asked Gautama.

"It is something that comes to all who live a long time. Their bodies become tired and weak. Do not trouble your mind, Gautama. The man is only a beggar."

But Gautama was troubled. Was there nothing anyone could do for the old man? Gautama had many questions he wanted to ask, but he felt it would be of no use to ask them. He turned his horse about and rode home to his palace. At the dinner table he found it hard to talk. His wife and others of his household wondered why their Prince was so strangely quiet.

Again another day Gautama and his servant Channa rode forth into fresh green woodlands. But Gautama saw not their loveliness. His mind was picturing the sick man he had seen lying on the rock. He followed the path by which he had gone before, but no one was to be found. Behind the trees back of the path Gautama saw a small hut. He walked toward it, opened the door. There on the floor he saw a man lying as if asleep. Gautama tried to wake him. "What is wrong with the man?" asked Gautama.

"The man is dead," answered Channa.

"Why? What does 'dead' mean?" asked Gautama.

"I cannot tell you," said Channa. "It is the way of all men. But this man was only a beggar. Do not let your mind be troubled." Without a word Gautama turned, jumped upon his horse, and rode home. More questions filled his mind, but he knew no one to whom he could go to ask them.

Now his wife had arranged a party for that evening, and dancers and musicians were ready to entertain their Prince. But Gautama did not wish to watch the dancers. He went to his own room and spent the evening and night alone. His wife thought he was asleep, but Gautama was going over and over in his mind the questions that troubled him.

"Is there no one who cares when beggars are sick or when they die? Why must people suffer so? Can't living be made happier somehow? I must go out into the bigger world—away from this palace where I'm always protected —and I must learn for myself what it really means to live."

In the early morning while it was still dark and the dancers and the royal family were still asleep, Gautama rose from his couch, determined to leave his palace home once and for all. He called his servant Channa to saddle his horse.

Gautama slipped quietly to the door of his wife's room. A little lamp gave a dim light. She lay asleep with her hand resting on the baby's head. Gautama longed to kiss them both, but he held back.

"If I kiss them, they will waken. She will try to prevent my leaving. I must go without her knowing."

Prince Gautama, for whom a crown and a kingdom were waiting, had decided not to be a king at all. He was determined to find out for himself the answers to the questions he still could not answer. Why do men become sick? Why do men become old? Why must everyone die? Why do we live at all?

By being hungry Prince Gautama was going to learn how it feels to be hungry. By taking care of the sick and the dying, he was going to learn what it means to be sick and to die. By being poor, he was going to learn how it feels to be poor.

So Prince Gautama, who had always slept on a cushioned couch behind guarded walls, was now going to sleep on the ground near the wild animals of the forests. Prince Gautama, on whose table the most delicious foods had been served in abundance, was now going to beg from door to door and to cook for himself one plain meal a day.

Sometimes he lived all alone. Sometimes he lived with other poor men who were also trying to find the answers Gautama wanted to find. Months and years passed by. Slowly he learned how to be at peace with himself. He learned not to be afraid of dying. He learned what seemed to him to be the true way of life.

By learning this peace of mind for himself, Gautama helped others also to find this same kind of peace. The people said:

"Before Gautama taught us, we were like men groping their way in the dark. Now we can see. Let us no longer call him just Gautama. Let us call him Gautama, the Buddha." In India the word Buddha means "one who has found a light." But the light that Buddha found was not the kind of light that one can see with one's eyes. His was an inward light that makes one's thinking clear and one's feelings peaceful.

Today, Gautama is usually called just Buddha. Millions of men and women the world over honor and love Buddha in much the same way as Jesus is honored and loved.

The Fig Seed

A Story from India

ONCE UPON A TIME in the very long ago the boy, Svetakatu,[1] lived in India. He was the oldest son of a wise and good man. When Svetakatu was twelve years old his father said to him:

"My son, you are now old enough to go away from home to school. I want you to live for a while with a certain famous teacher whom I know. There are many things to learn that you have not yet even heard of. I want you to learn to ask questions about matters that are hard to understand. I want you to learn how to think with your own mind while you listen to other people's thoughts. Svetakatu, some day you should be a teacher yourself."

So Svetakatu left home and lived for several years in the school of one of the great teachers of India. While he was away he read from the great books. He learned by

---

[1] Pronounced Svä-tä-kä'-tu.

heart many long prayers. He learned to sing the great songs of praise to God.[2]

Finally, after learning all he thought he needed to know, Svetakatu returned home. His father was more than happy to see his son again. But as they talked together, the father noticed how proud Svetakatu was of himself. The boy thought he knew more than his father. Svetakatu thought he knew all there was to learn! The father was puzzled. He thought: "How can I help my boy to realize how little he really knows?"

One day the two went for a stroll in the country. They came to a grove of fig trees and sat down together on some rocks on the bank of a river. After a short while the father said to Svetakatu:

"My son, since you now think you have learned so much and you are proud and conceited, I want to ask you a question. Have you learned how something that has *never* been heard *can* be heard? Or have you learned how something that has *never* been thought of *can* be thought of? Have you learned how something that has *never* been understood *can* be understood?" Svetakatu replied:

"No, father, tell me how." So the father said:

"I will teach you, my son. Bring me a fig from that fig tree." The son rose and picked a fig from the tree and brought it to his father.

"Here it is, sir."

"Cut it open," said his father.

"I have cut it open," said the son.

"What do you see there?"

"Oh, some small seeds, sir."

---

[2] The people of India say Brahman instead of God .

"Cut one of the seeds open."

"I have cut one open, sir."

"What do you see there?"

"Nothing, sir."

"Now, Svetakatu, you know that there must be something there. You know that this great fig tree here grew from just such a little seed."

"Yes, father, I know."

"Then did the tree grow from nothing?"

"It must be," said Svetakatu.

"You mean, Svetakatu, that what is alive, that made the great tree grow and bear figs, you cannot see?"

"It must be so," said the son.

"Then you should know also, Svetakatu, that not just in the fig seed, but everywhere, there is that which is alive which no one can see. The fig tree could never have grown without the life in that seed. And that life is invisible. You cannot see it. Nothing in the world can be without that invisible and living part from which it comes.

"Svetakatu, my son, the Invisible everywhere in the world is the divine in the world. It is God. It is Spirit. It is Life—it *is your* life." Svetakatu no longer felt proud and conceited. He wished he knew how to ask his father more questions.

"Oh, father," he begged, "help me understand even more."

"It shall be so, my son," said the father. "There is much more to learn."

The Lump of Salt

A Story from India

AGAIN SVETAKATU AND HIS FATHER went for a walk and
sat down together on some rocks in a grove of fig trees.
This time the father had brought with him an empty pan,
and hidden in a pocket in his gown he carried a lump of
salt. With the pan and the salt he was ready to give his son
another lesson.

"Why did you bring that empty pan along, father?"
asked Svetakatu.

"You will see, my son. I want you first of all to carry
it down to the river and fill it with water and bring it back
up here."

Svetakatu did as his father had asked. Pulling the lump
of salt out of his pocket, the father then said:

"Take this lump of salt, Svetakatu, and place it in this
pan of water."

They both watched and waited for a while after Svetakatu had dropped the salt into the pan.

"Now, Svetakatu," said the father, "I want that lump of salt back. Please pick it up and hand it to me."

"But, father, I do not see it any more."

"Put your mouth down into this end of the pan and taste the water," said the father, "and tell me, how it tastes there." Svetakatu put his mouth down into the water.

"The water tastes salty." That was all he could say. The father said:

"My son, take a sip at the farther end of the pan. How does it taste there?"

"It is salty there, also."

"Put your mouth into the middle of the pan, and taste it. How is it there?"

"It is salty there, also."

"You say it is salty, my son, and yet you say you cannot see any salt?"

"No sir, I can see none at all."

"My son," said the father, "even though your eyes do not help you to see any salt, yet with your tongue you can taste the salt, and you have found that what was before just a small lump of salt is now in this side of the pan of water. It is also in the middle and it is even at the farther end. It is everywhere in the water.

"Now, Svetakatu, my son, you should know also that, although your eyes do not help you to see God, yet there are other ways you may use to find out whether or not God is. God, like the salt, is everywhere—here, there and far off. As the salt is hidden in the water, so is God hidden in all the world. God is spirit, as you yourself are spirit. God is hidden in you, my son. God *is* you and you are part of

God." Svetakatu was quiet a long time. He was saying to himself over and over what his father had said:

"God is everywhere—here, there and far off.

"As the salt is hidden in the water, so is God hidden in all the world.

"God is spirit, as you yourself are spirit.

"God is hidden in you.

"God *is* you and you are part of God."

Finally Svetakatu said:

"Father, help me to understand even more."

"It shall be so, my son," said the father. "There is much more to learn."

The Questions of King Milinda

A Story from India

LONG, LONG AGO in Bactria, there was a very unusual king. His real name was King Milinda, but far more often he was called the king-who-is-always-asking-questions.

King Milinda asked questions of his nobles. He asked questions of visitors who came to his palace. He asked questions of his queen. Sometimes he even asked questions of his children. King Milinda was always asking questions. And the questions he asked were always difficult to answer. Finally, one day a courtier said:

"Your Majesty, why do you not go to see Nagasena [1] and ask your questions of him?"

"And who is this Nagasena?" said King Milinda. "I have never heard of him." The courtier answered:

"Nagasena, your Majesty, is said to be one of the wisest men of India. Have you not heard of his famous school? Hundreds of men from all over India—and even from other

---

[1] Pronounced Nā-gā-sé-na.

lands—have gone to live with Nagasena in his school in order that they may learn from him."

"India is many miles away," said King Milinda. "How can I leave my people and go so far off? It would take a month to make the journey. Traveling is dangerous. Do you really think that Nagasena is wiser than all the teachers of Bactria?" The courtier answered:

"I cannot say, your Majesty. I know only what travelers from India have said."

All day long King Milinda thought about the idea. At nighttime he dreamed about it. With each day that passed, he became more and more curious. If there was a man anywhere in the world who could answer his questions he would go to him no matter how far away the wise man might be.

So one bright morning, King Milinda and a band of his noblemen stepped into their chariots, whipped their horses, and off they went toward the wonderful land of India to see the great Nagasena. Day after day and week after week they rode. Neither cold nor heat, neither wind nor rain held them back.

Finally, one bright morning in the middle of the hot summer, they all arrived at Nagasena's school. Leaving their chariots and horses outside the gate, they entered the garden. There they found Nagasena with a large group of his students around him, sitting on the grass under the shade of a wide-spreading banyan tree.

King Milinda and his men at first stood quietly to one side and waited. But it was not long before Nagasena noticed them. Immediately he rose and greeted his guests. He invited them to sit down on the grass and join in the talk.

At this King Milinda was very happy. Before long out came one of his questions. He said:

"Noble sir, for many months we have been talking about Nagasena. We have spoken your name a hundred times a day. Over and over we have wondered: 'Is Nagasena a real person? Or is he just a name?' Now I must ask you, are you the same as your name? Or is your name one thing and are you something different from your name?" Then the wise man answered:

"Your Majesty, the name I am called by is Nagasena. It is the name my mother and father gave me when I was born. My friends say: 'Nagasena says this. Nagasena does that.' Yet, the truth is that my name and I are not the same." King Milinda then asked his second question.

"My noble teacher, you say you are not the same as your name. Does this mean, then, that you are not Nagasena? Is there no Nagasena? If you are not your name, who are you? Are you the same as the hair on your head?"

At this everybody laughed. What a foolish question! That is, everybody laughed except Nagasena. He liked the King Milinda. He liked him for trying so hard to think. Nagasena answered King Milinda very simply. He said:

"No, O King, I am not my hair."

"Are your bones you, then, O Nagasena?"

"No, O King, I am not my bones."

"Surely you are not your teeth and your fingernails, are you?" With this question all the men on the grass threw back their heads and roared with laughter. Nagasena waited and then answered:

"No, O King, I am not my teeth or my fingernails."

"Is your heart you, O Nagasena? Is your stomach you?

Is your brain you?" To all these questions and many more like them, Nagasena answered:

"No, O King, I am none of these things."

"But, Nagasena, are you not all of these parts of your body put together?"

"No, King Milinda, even all these parts of my body put together do not make me."

"Well, then," said the King, "are you something different from all these parts of your body?" Again Nagasena answered:

"No." Now King Milinda was really puzzled. He said:

"Noble teacher, I have asked you every question I can think of, but somehow I cannot find *you!* Where are *you?* Surely, you cannot mean there is no *you* at all. I cannot think that is the truth."

"You have spoken well, O King. I am here. I am real. I am not my name. I am not the sound of a word. Neither am I the different parts of my body. I am not the same as my whole body put together.

"King Milinda, I am not anything you can touch with your hands. You cannot see me with your eyes. Yet you know and I know that *I am.* But *what I am* is beyond our knowing."

Then King Milinda and all the men sitting around on the grass applauded their wise teacher. They said: "It is wonderful how he answers!" And King Milinda said to his companions:

"I am glad we came. Being here is better than I had hoped for. Let us find lodgings for tonight. Tomorrow I must ask more questions."

Wonders of Birth and Mysteries of Death

The next three stories are about three very famous babies. Jesus, Buddha and Confucius were born, lived to be men, and died many hundreds of years ago. Millions of people still honor these three men, and talk about them, and even love them, although nobody now can know them except by knowing the stories told about them.

Everybody likes to hear about such great persons, and storytellers have liked to tell their stories. But in those times long ago, when these three men lived, there were few books. Stories were not often written down. They were passed along from person to person by telling. Sometimes parts of the stories were forgotten, and the storyteller filled in the story as best he knew how. Sometimes, if a storyteller admired the great man a very great deal, in his enthusiasm he might exaggerate a little in the telling of a happening, without even meaning to do so.

In those olden times, the storytellers liked especially to tell about these men when they were babies. What happened when they were born seemed very important. In those olden times, some used to think:

"This great man was so very wise and good, he must have been a wonder as a baby. Or he must have had an unusually great mother." Others long ago said:

"Perhaps this great man was born into the world in a way

different from all other babies." It seems strange to us now that anyone could think anything could be more wonderful than the way a baby is really born and grows. But they did. Others long ago, who believed that angels and star people are real, said:

"The angels must have sung or played beautiful music while that little baby was being born. All the world and all the stars must have been happy." Others long ago, who believed that animals could talk and think like people, said:

"Even the animals must have been happy and gentle the night that child was born."

These are all old ways of thinking. And these next three stories are full of these old thoughts. Most of us today realize that such stories as these three birthday stories cannot be really, really true, yet many of us still like to hear them. Why? Because the stories remind us that these three great and good men, Jesus, Buddha and Confucius, were admired and loved and honored long ago as well as now.

The stories also remind us that long ago people loved newborn babies as much as we do, and felt that nothing could be too wonderful to have happened to a baby that grew to be a good and noble person. If angels could be true and if they could sing in the sky, we, too, would like to have them celebrate the birthdays of these three men, Jesus, Buddha and Confucius.

The Birth of Jesus

A Story from Palestine

NEARLY TWO THOUSAND years ago Jesus was born in Palestine far across the sea. Many wonder stories have been told about his birthday. This is the oldest of them all.

Mary, the young Jewish woman who became Jesus' mother, was beautiful to look at, and a favorite among her neighbors. If someone had hunted the world over, it is believed that he could not have found a finer woman than Mary—one whose mind was so empty of all ugly and mean thoughts and whose heart was so full of kindness for everyone.

Late one afternoon, as Mary sat in her garden dreaming of the time when she would become a mother, she thought she saw someone, unlike anyone she had ever seen before. He had flown like a bird with wings down into her garden and was standing before her. A light beamed about his face and his garments shone with the beautiful colors of the rainbow.

"Happy woman! Happy woman!" said the angel softly. He even called her by her name. "Mary," he said, "you will soon have a child. He shall be a boy. You shall call his name Jesus. When he is grown he shall be a King. His kingdom shall never be destroyed or come to an end."

When these soft words had been said, the shining angel disappeared, and Mary was left alone, trembling with wonder at this thing which was to happen to her.

Months passed by. The baby that rested in Mary's body had grown almost, but not quite, large enough to be born. Just at this time an order came from the governor saying that Mary and Joseph, her husband, would have to go to the town of Bethlehem to take care of their taxes. This

meant a journey of three or four days. Most of the time Mary could ride their little donkey. That would help, but Joseph would have to walk all the long way.

At last, late one evening, the hard journey was almost over. Mary and Joseph were nearing the town of Bethlehem. As they climbed the hill up to the town, they were happy in the thought that soon they would be able to wash their dusty hands and feet and lie down in a quiet room to sleep.

Without delay, they went to the well-known Bethlehem Inn and asked for a room. But the inn was already crowded with people. There was not a single empty room. Even the courtyard was jammed with camels and donkeys and bundles and a noisy crowd of people. Where could Mary and Joseph go? Joseph walked about exploring every nook and corner and asking from house to house. He knew that Mary was even more tired than he, and that she must have some place where she might lie down.

At last, he found a small place that was but half a room built against a hillside and open to the road. In it were two cows munching hay from the mangers in front of them. Could the travelers make use of this place and sleep with the animals? It would give them at least some cover and protection from the cold wind. They would try it.

So Mary lighted a couple of small oil lamps and placed them in niches in the wall so that she and her husband might see what they were doing. With the flickering light from these tiny lamps, the young couple made beds of straw on the hard mud floor. And tired as they could be, they lay down, covered themselves with a sheepskin blanket and tried to sleep.

Alongside them lay the cows, peacefully chewing the cud. Outside, high in the dark sky, thousands of bright stars beamed down upon them.

But the night was not far gone when Mary was wakened. She knew the time had come for her baby to be born. Joseph arose and busied himself at once to make her as comfortable as possible. But where would he put the new baby when it came? There was no time to spare. Joseph was thinking fast. He looked at one of the cow's mangers on the floor near Mary's bed. This would have to be the crib.

Joseph smoothed the hay still left in the manger. On top he spread out a soft piece of sheepskin for a blanket. When the new baby was born, Joseph wrapped it up and laid it gently in this manger crib. Before long the babe was sleeping snug and warm under the soft blanket, while Mary, his mother, lay beside him, her heart brimful of peace.

THE VISIT OF THE SHEPHERDS

Now that very night, in an open field out on a hillside a mile or so from the town, a few shepherds were sitting around a blazing fire. Some were sleeping while others kept sharp watch of every moving thing on the hillside lest a wolf or a bear sneak up in the dark and climb the wall into the sheepfold.

But it was not a wolf or a bear that surprised these shepherds that night. A shining angel suddenly flew down from the sky and lighted on the ground beside them. On seeing him, the shepherds screamed with fright.

"Be not afraid," said the angel softly, "for I have come to bring you good news that will make glad all the peoples of the world. This night a child has been born in Bethlehem, who is going to be that great person you have all been hoping would some day free your nation and bring you peace. This child shall be your King."

While the angel was still speaking to the shepherds, the sky began to glow with light. Instead of one angel, there appeared high in the sky many angels, and all began singing together. The beautiful chorus seemed to fill the whole wide sky. And the words of the angels' song sounded clear and strong.

"Glory to God in the highest! Glory to God in the highest!" the angels sang. "And on earth peace and good will among men."

As soon as the song was ended, the angels disappeared just as suddenly as they had come. The shepherds were once more left sitting alone in the darkness around the fire. Nothing else seemed important to them now except to go at once and see this thing that the angels had said had happened. The child must be somewhere in Bethlehem. They must find him.

Forgetting everything else—even their sheep and the wild beasts that might break into the fold—the shepherds hurried off to Bethlehem. Nor was it difficult, when once they were in the town, to find the little half-room on the hillside opening onto the road. Perhaps it was the flickering lights from the two small lamps that pointed the way. Perhaps it was the sight of Joseph moving about doing this and that for Mary and the babe. Perhaps it was the thin little cry of the newborn babe that gave them the hint.

But how surprised they were to find cows and the mother side by side and the baby lying in a manger crib! Could this

really be the babe who would some day be a King! It
seemed impossible, yet they felt it was true.

The shepherds told Joseph and Mary the whole story of
what had happened to them as they were keeping watch
over their sheep. The two listened and wondered at the
things the shepherds said.

When at last the men were satisfied that they had really
seen the wonder child, they left to go back to the hillside
and to their sheep. When once outside the quiet, sleeping
town, they sang their hearts out for joy.

Long after the shepherds had gone, Mary kept thinking
again and again of the story they had told. Over and over
she said to herself the words: "Peace on earth and good will
among men." Would her little boy some day really make
these things come true?

THE STAR IN THE SKY

In a country far off, three wise men were sitting together
upon the roof of their house, looking up at the stars in the
sky. Night after night for years, they had been studying the
skies in this same way. Many of the stars were like old
friends to them. These wise men knew all the stars that
always stayed in clusters and they knew equally well those
other stars (or planets, as we call them) that move more
quickly and alone across the sky.

In times long ago it was thought to be very important
to study the stars, because people believed that God put the
stars in their places in the sky in order to tell people on the
earth about important things that were going to happen. If
a new star appeared in the sky, one that the wise men had

never seen before, they immediately thought that something new and important had just happened or was about to happen on the earth.

That night, as these three wise men were sitting on the roof watching the sky, they saw a new bright star where they had never seen such a star before.

"What can this star mean?" they asked. "Something important has just happened somewhere on the earth. What can it be? Where has it happened?"

"I know," said one of the three wise men finally. "A child has been born who is going to be a very great and good man."

"But who can the child be? And where has he been born?" The three wise men talked about it long into the night. At last they came to this conclusion. "The child who has been born is going to become the King of the Jews. He will be that greatest of all Kings for whom the Jews have long been hoping—the King who will bring peace everywhere."

Now when once the men felt sure, their next thought was that they must go at once to Palestine and search for this child until they found him. That very night each one of the three men decided on the kind of present he would take to give to the new baby.

The next morning, they filled many bundles with food and supplies for a long journey. Toward evening they saddled their camels, hoisted their bundles and themselves up on to the camels' backs and off they went, toward the west in the direction of the land of Palestine.

It was no short or easy journey across miles of hot desert sands. During the heat of the daytime they set up a tent and rested under its shade. During the coolness of the night they rode forward with the bright stars to give them light.

Every night they watched for the special new star they had seen from their own roof top. And every night the star came out, like a cheerful companion on their long and lonely journey. The strange thing about that star was that each night it seemed to move along just a little ahead of them as if it were pointing in the direction in which they should go. So the three men rode along on their camels, believing they were being led by the star.

Finally, strange as it seems, when the men reached the town of Bethlehem, the star seemed to stop moving, and to hang still in the sky just over the little town. And, stranger still, the star seemed to hang directly over a certain house on a certain street. The three wise men believed they had found the right place, knocked on the door, and Joseph welcomed them in.

Immediately on seeing the little babe lying in his mother's arms, the three men fell on their knees before them and began to thank God. One by one, each pulled from a bag hanging to his belt the gift which he had brought. The first gave the baby a piece of gold. The second pulled out a package of incense that would make a sweet smell when it burned. And the third gave the babe some perfume. Mary and Joseph could scarcely believe what their eyes saw. They could not find the words they felt like saying. All they could do was to ask:

"Who are you? Where have you come from? Why are you doing these things?" Then Mary and Joseph heard the wonderful story of the new star that the men had seen in the sky and how it had guided them all the way to Bethlehem.

Although the strangers had much to tell, their visit seemed very short. Mary and Joseph were still in a daze as they stood in the doorway and watched the three men on their three camels pass down the street and out of sight.

When indoors and alone with their babe, the two could talk again. Did not the strangers know that Joseph was just a poor carpenter? And that Mary was only the daughter of a village farmer? How could their baby ever be a King?

This, then, is the old, old wonder tale about the birth of Jesus. What really happened no one can now know.

We do know, however, that this child of Mary and Joseph never became a King. Nor did he ever wish to be made a King. Jesus was a poor man by choice. When he was grown, he did not even have a home he could call his own. He was a teacher who traveled from town to town, teaching people how to live and what being good and doing right ought to mean.

Most of those who lived in that long-ago time have been forgotten, but Jesus is still remembered. Millions of people the world over still talk about Jesus. There are a great many people who even think about Jesus every single day. Stories Jesus told almost two thousand years ago are still being told, both to grownups and to children. There are a great many people who think that Jesus was greater than any King who ever lived. They think Jesus was great and good—even as good as God. Jesus' birthday is still celebrated. It is called Christmas Day, which means the birthday of the King.

The Birth of Buddha

A Story from India

THIS IS THE WONDER TALE about the birth of **Buddha**. It is an older story than the one about the birth of Jesus.

Buddha's mother was a Queen who lived in a grand palace in the faraway country of India. It was summer time. For almost a week the King and Queen and all the people of their land had been celebrating the annual summer festival. Each evening hundreds of men and women had gathered in the King's palace gardens to dance and be happy. Daily the King and Queen, sitting each on a royal chair hoisted on the shoulders of strong men, had been carried in procession through the streets of the city. All the while musicians made music with harps and drums and the people crowded about their rulers singing and throwing garlands of flowers into the royal chairs. And many were the gifts that the King and Queen gave away in return. The people said:

"Our Queen Maya is beautiful as a water lily, and as pure in her thoughts as the white lotus flower."

At the end of the last day of the festival, the tired Queen went to her own room and lay down on her couch to rest. Soon she was fast asleep and dreaming.

She dreamed that four beautiful and strong angels were lifting her up from her couch and carrying her off. Higher and higher they flew with her, until they were near the top of a very great mountain.

The angels showed her a palace gleaming like gold. They led her up its marble steps. They showed her through one beautiful room after another until finally she came to a bedroom that seemed to have been made just for her.

In her dream, she heard the angels tell her to lie down on the couch to rest. Presently, she saw a pure white elephant quietly enter the room. Gentle as an angel he seemed as he came up to her couch and stood beside her. On the end of his trunk he carried a large lotus flower, white as the cleanest snow, and he gave it to the Queen.

That very moment when the Queen took the flower, the room was filled with a heavenly light. In her dream she heard a terrific earthquake. Even the deaf heard the great roar, and the blind were suddenly able to see. Men who had been dumb and unable to speak began at once to talk together. Lame persons rose from their beds and walked. Beautiful music was heard everywhere. Harps played without anyone touching the strings. Trees at once began to blossom with new flowers. Lotus buds of all colors burst into bloom everywhere. Even the wild animals became gentle. None roared or howled or frightened children anywhere.

In the morning when the Queen awoke from her dream, she found herself in bed in her own palace as if nothing had happened. At once, she told the King the story of her dream, and the two were filled with wondering. The King said:

"I will call my sixty-four counselors immediately."

The sixty-four counselors hurried at once to the palace. The King welcomed them with refreshments of rice and honey, and told them his wife's dream.

"What does the dream mean? What is it that is going to happen?" he asked. The chief counselor answered:

"Do not be anxious, O King! The dream is a good one.

Your Queen is going to have a baby boy. When he is grown this child will either be King in your place or he will become a great teacher who will teach the people of many countries to know what they do not now understand. He will free them from their evil ways and will lead them to live in peace."

When the King heard these words from his chief counselor, he was very pleased, for the King did not yet have a boy child who could be taught to become a King.

Months afterwards, when the good Queen Maya realized that her baby would soon be born, she said to her husband:

"O King, I wish to go to the city of my parents."

Since the King wished to please his Queen, he consented, and ordered that her royal chair be made ready for her. He chose the strongest and best of his servants to take her safely to her mother's home.

The royal procession had gone but halfway to the Queen's former home, when they passed by a most beautiful park. On catching sight of the masses of flowers among the trees, Maya the Queen insisted that she must get down out of her chair and spend a while walking through the grove. She wanted to stand under the trees and to breathe in the sweet perfume of their flowers.

Queen Maya walked into the beautiful grove. She felt like singing with the birds that flitted about her. She had never before seen a lovelier spot.

A whole hour passed, but it seemed scarcely more than a few moments. Queen Maya began to feel that her baby was soon going to be born.

Quickly a couch was prepared for her and a curtain

thrown around her. When the baby was born, four angels appeared holding in their hands the four corners of a golden net. Into this net the baby was laid as if in a cradle. The angels spoke sweetly to the mother, and said:

"Be joyful, O Lady. A mighty son is born to you."

Presently four kings stood beside the four angels, and the angels gave the newborn child into the hands of the four kings. They in turn laid the child down on an antelope's skin that was soft to the touch. Before long the mother thought she saw her babe lift himself up on his feet. He stood for a moment and looked around in all directions. He even took one step and another and another until he had walked seven steps. All the while one angel held a white umbrella over him and the other angels laid garlands of flowers before him.

Then the child lay down again upon his antelope blanket and soon fell asleep just like any other small baby.

As servants carried the mother and babe back to the palace angels sang above them in the sky. The King, hearing the strange music, ran to meet his Queen. When he saw his newborn boy child he danced for gladness. The King's greatest wish had come true. He had a son! A Prince had been born who would some day rule the kingdom of the Sakyas! And the King called his son's name Siddhartha Gautama.

But the young child never did become a King. When he was old enough to choose for himself, he decided there was something more important for him to do than to be a King. He felt he could not learn what he needed to know if he stayed on in a rich King's palace. He wanted to know how it feels to be poor and hungry, and to work for one's own food.

So in the darkness of night the young Prince fled from the palace, taking with him nothing but the clothes he had on. Even these clothes he soon exchanged for the clothes of a beggar. Walking from town to town, begging his food in the streets, sleeping in the woods, he hunted for men who were thought to be wise. He asked them questions. He also spent hours sitting alone in the shade of the forest thinking. He wondered about sickness and about dying, about what happens after dying and what happens before one is born.

So it came about after some years that this young man became wiser than those who tried to teach him. Even to-day, after two thousand five hundred years, the name of this man is honored every day by millions of people.

But he is not called by the name that his father gave him. He is called the Buddha. This name means "the man with a light." But the Light that Buddha had was no ordinary light such as the light of a lamp. His Light was for the heart and for the mind. His Light is not the kind that eyes can see. Nor is his Light the kind that burns the fingers. Buddha's Light you can feel only with your heart when you know you are at peace with yourself. Buddha's Light is the Light of Truth.

The Birth of Confucius

A Story from China

THE MAN WHO BECAME the father of Confucius was called Kung the Tall because he towered head and shoulders above everyone else in his village. Kung the Tall lived in China a very long time ago. Kung the Tall was living in China when Buddha was born in India.

When this story begins Kung the Tall was an old man. As he thought back over the years of his long life he knew he ought to feel contented. He had been honored for his bravery as a soldier. He had been ruler of the people of his district. He had a faithful wife and a large family of nine children. He had enough money so that he could live comfortably, and he was highly respected by all who knew him. Yet Kung the Tall was a disappointed man.

His one most important wish had never come true. Kung was not happy. This was because all his nine children were girls, and Kung the Tall had no son to be company for him or to carry on the family name after his death.

But now the old man had a new wife—beautiful and young. Perhaps even yet Kung the Tall might have a boy child. He had not given up hope. And all his neighbors and all his friends were also hoping.

"If Kung the Tall does have a son, that child will someday be a great man"—this was what everybody was saying. This was what everybody was wishing for, and none wished harder than Kung's young wife.

Every day she made a wish for a boy child, and day by day she did what she could to make her wish come true. But she believed that somehow a child is always a gift from the Creator of all Life. So Kung's wife made her wish into a prayer to God. She even climbed to the top of a high mountain to make her prayer. Perhaps she felt nearer to the Creator when she could stand and look up at the wide, blue sky above and then look down on the broad, green earth below.

Kung's wife returned home and waited patiently week after week. Before long she could feel the baby moving inside her body, and she was happy.

One evening as she was sitting alone in her garden in the dimness of the moonlight, she had a surprising dream. She saw a little animal coming towards her. It was not a goat, nor was it a sheep or a dog. The animals' body shone in the moonlight. Its tail spread out like a fan and on its head was one turned-up horn! Could it really be a Unicorn? Surely only in storybooks was such an animal ever seen!

Kung's wife threw a small silk scarf over the animal's one horn just to see if it were really there. Yes, it was there, and it had in its mouth a long piece of jade. Kung's wife wondered.

The Unicorn came closer until Kung's wife could reach out her hand and take the stone tablet from its mouth. Her hands trembled as she tried to read the words that had been carved into the jade:

"A son of the Great Spirit is to be born. Someday he shall rule the land of Chou as a good and wise King."

Kung's wife was frightened. She looked up to ask the Unicorn what the words might mean, but the strange animal was gone. Kung's wife was left alone in her garden in the moonlight. She awoke trembling with wonder at what she had seen.

Not many weeks after this the longed-for day came. It was evening. Kung the Tall and his young wife were waiting for the final moment when their child would be born. In the garden outside the little cottage some of their friends were also waiting and hoping, moment by moment, for the good news.

Then they, too, had a surprise. High above them they saw two great dragons curling their long snakelike bodies in and out among the clouds. Their fiery eyes turned this way and that as if they were watching the people on the earth. Said one of the waiting friends:

"Surely these good dragons are keeping guard over the blessed mother and over the child about to be born."

And beside the two long, fiery-eyed dragons, five old but wondrous men appeared in the sky, walking upon the clouds. Said one of the waiting friends:

"These five old men of the sky are the five immortals who never, never die. They have come down from the five planets to celebrate the birth of this great child."

And beside the two long, fiery-eyed dragons, and beside the five old men from the five planets, there appeared also in the sky among the soft clouds five musicians with pipes and harps in their hands, playing wondrous music and singing as they played. The words came down from the sky like the clear ringing of a bell:

"This night a child is born. He shall be a great King, who shall make good laws and shall help people to do the right."

When the young mother in the little Chinese home down below heard the sweet strains of the music, the piping and the singing, her waiting ended. Her boy child was born! To her it had all seemed much like a dream until she heard the voice of her husband:

"A son at last, my good wife. Now my happiness is full!" He lifted his newborn boy child and proudly laid him down in his mother's arms.

For a long while he sat by his wife's bed as the two of them looked in silence on the face of their young son. It was a homely face. But this did not matter to his happy parents. In their eyes he was a wonder child.

Presently, as they were fondling him, a strange writing seemed to show on the child's breast. Five Chinese characters! What could they mean?

Wiser ones than Kung the Tall were called into the room to read the writing. They were amazed when they saw the characters, for the words on the child's body were those of the heavenly song:

"This night a child is born. He shall be a great King who shall make good laws and shall help people to do the right."

So this is the very old story of the birth of Confucius. Kung-fu-tze, the Chinese say, meaning Kung the Master, or Kung the Teacher. We say Confucius for short.

But this Chinese boy child of long ago did not become a King. Instead he taught other men how to rule their people wisely. Confucius also taught that being able to rule oneself is more important than ruling others. So Confucius had wise words for everybody, big and little, rich and poor. Even after more than two thousand years millions of Chinese still honor Confucius and follow his teachings. All over the world he is regarded as one of the wisest and greatest teachers who has ever lived.

The Mustard-Seed Medicine

A Story from India

KISA GOTAMI [1] was a beautiful young woman with neither father nor mother to care for her. In the city market one day, a rich young man saw her as she stood in a booth selling flowers. He fell in love with her at first sight. Later he married her. Everyone thought: "What a happy life Kisa Gotami will now have!"

Some time after that a baby was born, a beautiful little boy, and Kisa Gotami was completely happy. The days slipped by very fast as she watched her little son grow and learn. Almost before she knew it, he could run about and talk. She loved him more than anyone else in all the world. She loved him when he was obedient and when he was stubborn. She loved him when he laughed and when he cried.

But one day the little boy suddenly became very sick. Even though his mother and father did everything they knew how to do for him, the little boy did not get well. In a few days he died.

---

[1] Pronounced Kē-sä Gō-tä-me.

Kisa Gotami could not believe her little boy was really dead. She thought his sickness had only put him to sleep. Some kind of medicine would surely wake him up. So she wrapped the little body in its baby sheet and lifted it up in her arms. She carried it to her neighbor's door.

"Please, my friend," she begged, "give me some medicine that will cure my child." But when her neighbor lifted the sheet and saw the baby's face, she shook her head sadly. She knew there was no medicine that could cure him.

Kisa Gotami was not easily discouraged. She went from door to door. She begged each neighbor she saw: "Please give me some medicine to cure my little boy." But each neighbor in turn looked at the baby's sleeping face and shook her head sadly. The neighbors all felt very sorry for Kisa Gotami. When she was gone, they said:

"Poor Kisa Gotami! Has she lost her senses?" Finally she met a man on the street who said:

"My good woman, I cannot give you any medicine for your child, but I know a man who can help you."

"Oh, tell me, please, who is he and where may I find him?"

"Go to Buddha," said the man encouragingly. "He can always help people." So Kisa Gotami hurried to the home of Buddha. She stood before the great man and said:

"Good Buddha, I am told you are always able to help people in trouble. Please give me some medicine that will cure my child."

Buddha looked tenderly at the anxious mother. He knew the child was dead. He knew he could not bring the dead back to life again, but he knew also that he could help the mother to feel peaceful and comforted.

"My good woman, you must help me find the medicine," said Buddha kindly. "Go and bring me a handful of mustard seed."

"Surely I can easily find a handful of mustard seed," said Kisa Gotami eagerly.

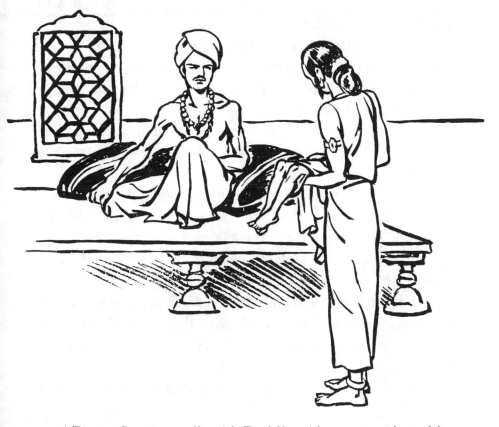

"Do as I tell you," said Buddha, "but remember this: The mustard seed must be taken from a house where no one has ever died or it will be of no use."

Believing she could find the mustard seed in some house where no one had ever died, Kisa Gotami thanked Buddha and went back home. There she gently laid her child's lifeless body on its little bed. Then she went out alone to find the handful of mustard seed.

First she went hopefully to her next-door neighbor. "Have you a handful of mustard seed?" she asked. "Buddha says it will cure my child."

"Certainly I have mustard seed. I will gladly give you a handful and more."

"Thank you so much, kind neighbor," said Kisa Gotami, "but before taking the seed I must ask you a question. Has anyone ever died in your house—a father or grandfather or grandmother or anyone else?"

"O Kisa dear, have you forgotten?" said the neighbor in surprise. "Our dear grandfather died here scarcely more than a year ago."

"Then your mustard seed cannot cure my child," said Kisa Gotami sadly. "Buddha said that I must find the seed in a home where no one has ever died."

Hopefully Kisa Gotami went to another house. She went from door to door, to every house in the village, asking for a handful of mustard seed. When she asked the question: "Has anyone ever died in this house?" one said:

"Yes, our oldest son died here. It was ten years ago, but we still miss him." Another said:

"Both our grandparents died in this house." Another said:

"My husband died here many years ago." At every door it was the same. Someone would say:

"Good woman, why remind us of our sorrow? How can you expect to find a house where no one has died? Don't you know that the living are few but the dead are many?"

At last, tired and discouraged, Kisa Gotami went outside the village and sat down alone on a rock under a banyan tree. She knew now that even Buddha had no medicine for her child. Nothing could bring him back to life again. Tears blinded her eyes. Although it was broad daylight, it seemed as though the darkness of night had fallen over her.

As she sat quietly under the banyan tree, she slowly began to feel peaceful. After all, she was not all alone and deserted. Nor did she feel that her little boy was all alone. The really real little boy she loved was gone. That was true. She did not know where he had gone or why he had gone, but she did know now that his body was dead. It had died, just as thousands of other persons' bodies had died before. Just as her own body would sometime die. Just as everybody in all the world must sometime die. Kisa Gotami felt that all people were together in dying. No one was ever all alone.

But Kisa Gotami wanted to talk with Buddha again. She was beginning to understand why he had sent her to get the handful of mustard seed. But she wanted him to tell her. So she arose and went back to his home. Buddha greeted her in the same gentle way he had done before.

"Good woman, have you brought the mustard seed?" he asked.

"No, my lord. There is no house in all the village where someone has not at sometime died."

"Sit down beside me," said Buddha. "Let us talk together a while." Kisa Gotami was glad to listen and be quiet.

"Our lives in this world are all short whether we live for

one year or for a hundred years. Everyone who is born must sometime die—yes, everyone. There are no exceptions. We all have our times of happiness and also our times of pain and sorrow. Do not try to free yourself from suffering. Try rather to free yourself from hate and selfishness.

"Do not struggle, good woman," said Buddha. "Be at peace. Accept your life as a gift. Take the days as they come one by one. Fill them as full of kindness as you can."

Kisa Gotami went often to Buddha. The thoughts that he gave her to think about were the best kind of medicine for her loneliness. Now that she knew how much it hurt to be lonely, she began to learn how to comfort others who also were sad.

Kisa Gotami, now a rich man's wife, went often to the homes of the poor. She brought them food. She played with their children. In these ways she slowly learned how to comfort herself.

A Musician

and His Trumpet

A Story from India

IN THE LONG, LONG AGO, a certain soldier went to Kassapa, another of the great teachers of India, with this question: "What is it that happens when a person dies?"

In order to answer the soldier's question, Kassapa told this story.

In olden times a certain musician, carrying his trumpet under his arm, stopped to rest on a bench in the market place of a small village. He laid his trumpet down on the ground beside him. Nobody else seemed to be anywhere around, for all the villagers were at home having supper.

Being lonely, the musician picked up his trumpet and began to play. He blew it three times, and then set it on the ground again beside him.

When the villagers heard the trumpet blowing, they were puzzled, for none of them had ever seen or heard a trumpet before. They said to one another:

"What is it that is making that charming and delightful sound?"

They rushed out of their houses and gathered in the market place. There they found the musician. They asked him:

"Sir, what was it that made that charming and delight-ful sound?"

"Friends, it was this trumpet that you see lying on the ground here beside me that made that sound."

One of the villagers then picked up the strange instru-ment which had been called a trumpet. He looked it all over. He put it down on the ground again so that it stood up on its large round end. He called to it:

"Speak, O Trumpet! Speak, O Trumpet!" But the trumpet did not make a sound. Another villager turned the trumpet over and put it down on its side. He also called:

"Speak, O Trumpet! Speak, O Trumpet!" But the

trumpet did not make a sound. Another man put the trumpet down on its other side and spoke to it. Another shook it this way and that way and called. The crowd began calling too:

"Speak, O Trumpet! Speak, O Trumpet!"

But no! The trumpet did not make a sound! The trumpeter smiled and thought to himself:

"How foolish these villagers are! How can they hope to hear the sound of the trumpet by trying other ways to play it than the right way?"

Finally, with the villagers watching him, the musician picked up the trumpet and again blew it three times. After this he walked off with the trumpet under his arm, and disappeared down the path.

The villagers were left to think things through for themselves. Everyone began talking at once. Finally, they agreed on the right answer to their puzzling. This is the way one of the men explained it:

"When the trumpet was connected with a person who blew his breath into it, it made a sound! But when the trumpet was not connected with a person and no breath was blown into it, then the trumpet made no sound at all."

Kassapa then turned to the soldier and said:

"It is precisely so with us and our bodies. When the body is not connected with Life then it can *not* walk forward or walk backward. It can *not* stand or sit or lie down. Then, too, it can *not* see things with its eyes, or smell things with its nose, or taste flavors with its tongue, or touch things with its hands. Then it can *not* understand with its mind. We say the person is dead.

"But when the body is connected with Life, the body *can* walk forward and backward. It *can* sit down and stand up and lie down. It *can* see things with its eyes, and hear things with its ears. It *can* smell with its nose, and taste with its tongue, and touch things with its hands. It *can* understand with its mind. We say the person is alive.

"When the Life and the body are together, there is a living person. When the Life is not connected with the body, the body is dead. It is just as helpless as a trumpet that has no musician to play it." The soldier then said to Kassapa, his teacher:

"What you have said seems clear to me and I understand, but I am still wondering. What is this Life that is sometimes in the body and sometimes not? Teach me more."

So the soldier stayed many days with his teacher. But the more he knew, the more there seemed left to wonder about.

The Road to
Olelpanti

A Story from North America

In the far-off beginning before there were any Indians living, there was another and very different race of men on the earth. For thousands of years this first race of men had been living together peacefully and happily. But as their numbers multiplied and the earth became crowded, these first people began to quarrel and fight. And Olelbis—The-Great-One-Who-Sits-Above-the-Sky—decided something must be done.

This is what he did. He turned the people one by one into other kinds of living creatures. Some he turned into trees and flowers; others he turned into birds and insects, and still others into land animals and fish. You might say only a handful of people were left. And all of these were old people who would soon die. Among them was Sedit, the Coyote man. The earth in time grew very beautiful with green grassy plains and wooded hills and rivers, where animals of all kinds and birds and fish lived without fear of human hunters.

But Olelbis—The-Great-One-Who-Sits-Above-the-Sky—was lonely without human beings on his world. So he thought out a new plan. He would create a new race of men. He would make the first man and woman come out of the first tree he had made. This time he wanted people to learn to live together happily and peacefully. How could he help them? Perhaps if he made them immortal they would be happy, he thought. "I will make them so that they will never have to die."

So Olelbis called the two Brothers Hus who lived with him in his beautiful Sky Land of Olelpanti and said to them: "Brothers Hus, I have a great work for you to do. Fly down to the world below where the first tree is growing. Soon I shall cause men and women to come forth out of that tree to live on the earth. But before this happens, you must build a road leading from the earth to Olelpanti. Gather great stones from the hillside and pile them one upon the other like steps leading up to the sky."

"For what purpose do you wish so great a work done, Olelbis?" asked the Brothers Hus.

"It is because I wish that the new race of men, whom I am about to bring forth from the ground, should never have to die. I desire that when they grow old they may be able to renew their youth. I shall, therefore, place two springs at the top of the road that you build, so that when a man grows old, he may climb up this road; and when he reaches the top, he may drink out of one spring and bathe in the other spring. Then his white hair will become dark again and his bent and crippled body will become strong and straight. If an old woman climbs up the road and drinks of the one spring and bathes in the other, she will come out a beautiful young girl. When these people grow old a second time, they may climb they road again and return young and strong to live anew. So shall the men of the earth live on and on forever."

When Olelbis finished speaking, the Brothers Hus said, "We will do as you have commanded us." So they gathered their tools, and spreading their wings they flew down to the earth to begin the work of building the road of stones.

By the end of the first day, they had piled the stones as high as a house. By the end of the second day, the road was as high as a tall tree. By the end of the third day, it was very high indeed. By the end of the sixth day, the road was touching the clouds. Yet it was still a long way from Olelpanti, and there was much more work to do.

A little before noon on the sixth day, as the Brothers Hus were working, they saw someone walking toward the beginning of the long road. He finally reached the place and sat down beside the road to watch the Brothers as they worked. They knew it was Sedit, the Coyote man, but they said nothing.

"What are you doing here?" Sedit finally asked. "Why are you building this road? It is a great deal of work, and does not seem to be leading anywhere. Can you tell me what it is that you are doing?"

"Olelbis has commanded us to build this road," said one of the Brothers. "Olelbis is planning to make a new race of men come out of the earth. Before he does, he wishes to have a road built reaching from the world to Olelpanti. At the top of the road Olelbis will place two springs."

"That seems strange," objected Sedit, the Coyote man. "There are springs enough on the earth. Why should there be more?"

The other Brother went on with the story. "Olelbis has plans for these springs. As men live on earth they grow old. When men grow old, they become weak and bent and unable to do their work. Olelbis does not wish them to grow old and die. So he plans that when men grow old, they can climb this road, and bathe in one spring and drink from the other. Then they will have their youth once more."

Sedit sat quietly for a time, thinking of what the Brothers had said. "Do you believe all this?" he asked at last.

The Brothers Hus were surprised. They had not thought of questioning the plan of Olelbis. But they were interested to know what Sedit meant. So they asked, "Why is it not a good plan?"

"What will people eat if nothing dies?" asked Sedit. "Deer will not die. Fish will not die. Men will not be able to kill anything. What will be left to eat? Nothing but acorns. How uninteresting it will be to live without hunting!"

The Brothers Hus began to be troubled. But Sedit had much more to say.

"I think it is better that men and women should marry and that new children should be born, than that old people should be made young. If they marry, the men will work for the women and the women will work for the men, and so they will help each other. If a man has a wife, he will catch fish and kill deer and bring them home and give them to his wife to cook. And if the woman has a child, her neighbors will say, 'There is a nice baby over there,' and they will go to see it. And so they may be glad together."

"But if someone dies, everyone will mourn and be sad," said the Brothers Hus. "That surely cannot be good."

"When a man grows old, let him die," said Sedit. "When a woman grows old let her die. When they die, the neighbors will come and say, 'A man has died,' or 'A woman has died.' Then they will make ready to help the relatives of the dead. I think this is better."

"Suppose," continued Sedit, "an old man goes up that road alone and comes back young. He is still alone just as before. They will have nothing to be glad about. They will never make friends. They will never have children. They will never have any fun in the world nor anything to do but to grow old and to go up that road and come back again young. It is not good."

The Brothers Hus had not thought of these things before. Yet the longer they thought, the more true Sedit's words seemed.

"Let us destroy the road that we have built," one Brother finally said to the other. "Let us fly back to tell Olelbis these things. Perhaps he may change his plans for men."

Then Sedit, the Coyote man, turned and walked away, satisfied that he had spoken truly. And the Brothers Hus prepared to fly back to Olelpanti. They pulled several large stones out from the bottom of the pile and the whole road fell, the stones scattering far and wide.

Then just as they were ready to take flight up to Olelpanti, one of the Brothers called back to Sedit.

"Of course, you know that this means that you too will die— just as every other living thing upon the earth will die."

"Come back! Come back!" screamed Sedit. "We must talk some more."

But the two Brothers flew off. Higher and higher they rose, circling above Sedit, until at last he could see them no more.

"What am I to do now? I wish I had not said so much," thought Sedit. "I wish I had not said anything. I do not want to die. What can I do?"

For some time Sedit stood looking around helplessly—till he saw some sunflower plants growing nearby.

"If everything on earth is going to die," said Sedit, "then I am not going to remain on earth. I will make wings for myself, and I will fly to Olelpanti where all living things last forever."

So Sedit picked the leaves off the sunflower plant. He fastened them together in the shape of two wings, and tied the wings to his shoulders. Then he lifted himself as a bird into the air. He flew a short way without any trouble, but the hot noonday sun began to dry the leaves, and one by one they wilted and dropped off. He tried to fly faster in order to reach Olelpanti before the leaves were all gone. But the leaves fell faster than he could fly. Then he felt himself falling. He landed on the pile of rocks which was to have been the road to Olelpanti and was crushed to death.

Olelbis, looking down from Olelpanti, saw all that had happened.

"It is his own fault," he said to the Brothers Hus who had just arrived at Olelpanti. "Sedit is the first of all living things to die. He has been killed by his own words. From this time on, all men will die. They will know the gladness of birth. They will know the sorrow of death. And through these two things together men will come to know love."

Human Universals

The Complaint against the Stomach

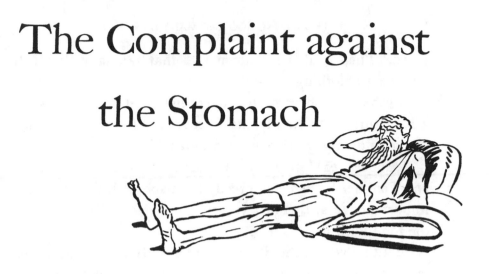

A Story from Greece

A CERTAIN MAN HAD A DREAM in which he heard his Hands and his Feet, his Mouth and his Teeth all scolding his Stomach.

"You are fat and lazy," said the Feet to the Stomach. "You get all the food and yet you do nothing. Think of all the walking *we* have to do, going back and forth to town to buy food. Yet in the end you, greedy Stomach, get all the food and we get nothing."

"We agree," said the Hands. "Think of all the hard work *we* do, hoeing and weeding the garden, gathering the food, cleaning it, cooking it and all that, and yet in the end we get nothing and you, greedy Stomach, get it all."

"Hear! Hear!" called the Mouth and Teeth and Tongue all together. "How could any food be bought in the market at all if it were not for us. After you Feet and Hands have finished your work, we take the food you give us. We chew it and mix it with saliva and prepare it, so that it can be enjoyed. Then it all slips down into that fat, lazy Stomach and we get nothing at all."

In the man's dream, the quarreling went on like this for a long time until finally the Feet said: "Let's all together refuse to do any work for the Stomach."

"Good idea!" cried the Hands and Mouth and Teeth and Tongue. "Then you, greedy Stomach, will find out how important we are. Then you will *have* to divide some of the food with us."

All this while, the Stomach lay quietly in a corner. He said nothing. He really was fat and round and he seemed very lazy and satisfied.

So the Feet and the Hands and the Mouth and the Teeth and the Tongue made an agreement with one another. The Feet promised not to walk. The Hands promised not to carry anything. The Mouth promised not to open and shut. The Teeth promised not to chew, and the Tongue promised not to talk.

Then it seemed as if morning had come. The man thought he had awakened but he was still asleep and dreaming. To his surprise he found he could not walk. He could not carry anything in his hands. He could not open his mouth. He could not chew or even talk. He felt very sick.

This condition seemed to last for several days. Each morning the man felt weaker and thinner. He did not know what to do, for he knew that if this sickness continued he would starve to death.

Finally after many days, the dreaming man saw his Feet and Hands and Mouth and Teeth and Tongue and Stomach all lying around on the floor scarcely able to move, and much less able to quarrel with one another.

He heard a weak small voice speak. It was one of his Feet trying to talk. "We must admit we have been foolish," said the Foot. "In his quiet way Stomach has been doing work for us all the time."

"How silly of us to think Stomach was lazy just because he was quiet," said the Tongue.

"Yes," said the Hands, "we thought Stomach here was getting all the food, but we see now that he had his own special ways of sending most of it back to us."

Stomach smiled when he heard his companions speaking in this way.

"Let's all begin working together again," said the Mouth and Teeth and Tongue all at once. Everybody agreed and the Man woke up.

To his surprise, he found his Feet could walk again. He found his Hands could carry things again. He found his Mouth could open and shut and his Teeth could chew and his Tongue could talk. The Man began to feel better right away.

As he ate his breakfast, he remembered his dreaming. He thought to himself, "Each part of my body needs every other part. They all work together—my Feet and Hands and Mouth and Teeth and Tongue and Stomach. If any one of them stops working, they all have to stop and I become sick. When each does what it knows how to do, I am well and strong. I can do things, too, and I am happy."

The Trees Choose a King

A Story from Palestine

IT IS SAID BY SOME that, long ago, the trees of the forest could talk, and if living things can talk, they can also quarrel. This is what happened once upon a time to the trees of the forest. They quarreled so often that they finally decided they must have a King to rule over them to keep them at peace.

At first almost every tree in the forest began thinking: "How wonderful it would be to be chosen King!" And many of the trees began boasting about themselves. "Let me be the King! Let me be the King! I would make the best King!" cried this tree and that tree all over the forest.

But one of the more thoughtful trees among them called out: "Stop and think! You can't be King and keep on doing what you do now. Whoever is chosen King will have to be willing to change his way of life. If you are a fruit tree you will have to stop using your strength to bear fruit on your branches. You will need to spend your strength growing high and strong so that you can wave your branches to and fro over us all. That's the only kind of tree that can keep us at peace together."

On hearing this, all the trees at once stopped their boasting and grew quiet and thoughtful. When they began talking again, they were serious, and asked one another:

"Which tree would really make the best King?"

They talked a long while before they could make a choice. Finally, they went to the Olive Tree and said:

"We want you to be our King." But the Olive Tree said:

"Why should I give up making fine-tasting olives in order to grow high and wave my branches to and fro over you all? My olives bring me great honor among men. No, I do not want to be your King." Then the trees went to the Fig Tree and said:

"We want you to be our King." But the Fig Tree said:

"Why should I give up bearing sweet figs in order to grow high and wave my branches to and fro over you all? My sweet figs keep the people of the world cheerful. I like to be praised for my fruit. No, I do not want to be your King." Then the trees went to the Grapevine and said: "We want you to be our King." But the Grapevine said:

"Why should I give up bearing my big juicy grapes in order to grow high and wave my branches to and fro over you all? The people of the world are made glad by my fruit. No, I do not want to be your King." The trees of the forest asked one tree after another. And one after another the trees all said:

"Why should we give up what we like to do? We want

to stay as we are." That is, they all refused except the little Thorn Bush who thought: "Perhaps now is my chance to be important. Nobody has ever noticed me before. I'd like to be different."

Sure enough, when the trees could find no good tree in the whole big forest that was willing to change its way of life in order to be their King, they went at last to the little Thorn Bush and they said:

"We want you to be our King."

At first the Thorn Bush thought it was a joke. "Do you really and truly want me to be your King?" he asked. All the trees said:

"Yes, really and truly we want you to be our King." The Thorn Bush chuckled and called with a loud voice:

"Come and crawl within my shadow, all ye trees of the forest and be safe! Do what I say and be at peace!"

Even while the Thorn Bush was speaking, it began to grow taller and taller until its thorny branches spread high and far over all the trees of the forest. Knowing then that he was big and powerful, the Thorn Bush called again with a sharp and cruel voice:

"Listen well to my words, all ye trees of the forest! You have chosen me to be your King. From now on you must obey me. If at any time any one of you refuses to do as I command, I shall call Man into the forest. Man is greater and stronger than all of us put together. I shall say to Man:

'Gather up from the ground all my dry and useless thorny branches. Make a fire of them, and burn up the whole forest.' "

All the trees of the forest were so frightened by what the Thorn Bush said that they have never quarreled since.

A Visit to the Land-of-Great-Men

A Story from China

LONG, LONG AGO some Chinese gentlemen became discontented with the way the people of their country acted. They decided to go together on a trip to find, if they could, a better country where the people were not silly and did not quarrel, and where they were good to one another. These dissatisfied gentlemen had heard rumors of a country called the "Land-of-Great-Men." What kind of a country was that? What were the people like? These Chinese were curious and decided to see for themselves.

So they hired a boat and set sail. Slowly, day after day, they sailed up the winding river until at last they came to the spot where they had been told to go ashore. Tang, their leader, said:

"The City-of-Great-Men is some miles inland from here on the other side of those hills." So the travelers set out to walk toward the city. The paths they came upon crossed and divided so often that the men were none too sure which path to follow, but fortunately they came to a small house standing in a grove of bamboo trees.

Tang was on the point of walking up to knock on the door, when an old man stepped out. And, to the great surprise of the travelers, he stood on a little rainbow-colored cloud about a foot above the ground.

As soon as he saw the company of strangers he stepped into his house, and in a moment appeared again at the door. Behind him came his wife, and each of them stood in the doorway upon a rainbow-colored cloud. They smiled at the strangers and bowed.

"Come in, good strangers, and rest yourselves under our humble roof," the old man said. The Chinese travelers bowed their "thank-you's" in return, but did not go into the house. The old man asked what country they had come from. When he learned they had come up the river all the way from China, he insisted that they must come in and rest and eat at his table.

Once more Tang thanked the old man and his wife for their kind hospitality, but begged to be allowed to go on into the City-of-Great-Men. "But before we go," said Tang, "may we ask you a question?"

"Certainly, certainly."

"Why is it, sir, that you and your wife each stand on a little cloud? Were you born with these clouds fastened to your feet?"

"Yes, these clouds stay beside us always."

"Does everybody in your country walk on a cloud?"

"Yes."

"Are all the clouds as beautiful as yours?" asked Tang.

"The color of our clouds we can do nothing about," said

the old man. "Of course, everyone prefers to have a rainbow-colored cloud. A yellow one is next best. Then come the red and green and blue clouds. But the grey and black clouds are the worst. Nobody wants one of them."

"Who, then, decides the color of the cloud you have?" Tang's questions were multiplying every minute.

"The color of one's cloud changes from time to time. It is always like your disposition," said the old man. "When you feel happy and kind toward people, your cloud is rainbow-colored. But when you feel ugly or quarrelsome or gloomy, your cloud becomes grey, or even black. The color of your cloud all depends on how you feel inside."

"How does the cloud know how you feel inside?" asked one of the younger Chinese.

"That's the strange part, my friends. You don't have to tell your cloud whether your feelings are kindhearted or nasty. The cloud just knows. And it changes its color without your asking. You can't do anything about it."

The strangers looked at one another in surprise.

"That's the most important thing about our country," the old man went on. "You can never hide your feelings. You can't fool people or pretend you are different from what you really are. Your cloud by its colors tells the truth to everyone you meet whether you want it to do so or not."

"I would be afraid to live in a country like this." The man who spoke turned as if he wanted to go home. "It would be a queer feeling to know that everybody could see just how you were feeling all the time."

"But wouldn't it be wonderful?" said another. "No cheating! No pretending! You would always know the truth."

"Well, I know I should always want my cloud to be rainbow-colored."

"That's the way we all feel about our clouds," said the old man.

"Do many people have black clouds?" asked a curious young fellow.

"You had better find out for yourselves," said the old man.

So Tang asked him the right path to take in going to the City-of-Great-Men. When Tang had been given his directions, he bowed and thanked the old man for his kindness, and the travelers turned and went on their way.

When once over the top of the hill, they could see the big city below them in the valley. As they came nearer, they could see that the houses were very much like their own houses at home. As they walked up the main street, they could see that it was crowded with people coming and going, buying and selling, just like their main street at home. The people they saw looked just like their own countrymen and were dressed just like themselves. There was one very big difference, however. Everyone was walking about on a little cloud that floated along a foot or so above the ground!

The strangers were fascinated by the many colors in the clouds. Blue, yellow, red, green and oh, there were so many, many clouds all the colors of the rainbow. It was a beautiful sight! Scarcely a black cloud anywhere. This was very surprising.

Presently a feeble old man passed by them. He was dressed in a ragged blue robe, holding out a cup begging for money. Yet even this beggar seemed happy, and was walking along on a lovely rainbow-colored cloud.

"How can this be?" all the Chinese wanted to ask at once.

"You see," said a man near by who belonged to the city, "our clouds pay no attention to whether we are rich or poor. It does not matter what kind of work we do either — whether one is a teacher or a peddler of pots and pans. It does not matter whether one owns a big house or a little one. It does not matter whether one is pretty or homely. The color of one's cloud depends on the kind of person one is inside. If one is feeling happy and kind and helpful, one's cloud is rainbow-colored. If one is feeling stingy or proud or cross or quarrelsome, one's cloud grows black."

"But I do not see black clouds anywhere around. How is that?" asked one of the travelers.

"That's because we all dislike black clouds. If you go about on a black cloud, nobody will buy the things you want to sell. Nobody will talk to you or do anything for you. But when everybody is good to everybody else, we're all friends."

While the conversation was going on, the travelers saw that the people on the street were stepping to the one or the other side of the road, and that the center was being left empty. Soon they heard bells ringing. Then the men ringing the bells came up the street, each on a rainbow-colored cloud. Next came two other men carrying two big painted signs on top of high poles. And behind these men walked a richly dressed man, under a big red umbrella carried by another man walking beside him. Many others followed in the procession and each was moving along on a little cloud. It was a fascinating sight.

But there was one thing wrong. The man under the big

red umbrella was walking on a cloud that was covered with a piece of red silk.

"Why is this?" asked Tang of their new-found friend.

"The truth is that this man is one of our most important officers, but his cloud is grey and he is trying to cover it up. But it's foolish for him to do this, for everybody knows the color of his cloud."

"This is not fair," called one of the Chinese.

"What do you mean?" asked Tang. "What's not fair?"

"I mean that it isn't fair that in our country we do not walk on clouds. Why has God given clouds to these people and left us without clouds? These clouds are very useful. When everybody has a cloud, it's very easy to tell who are good people and who are not."

"That is quite true," said another one of the Chinese, "but even in our own country where we have no clouds, we can pretty well tell the kind people from the selfish ones."

"That may be so," said the first man, "but sometimes people can pretend and they fool you. A smile on a face may cover up a cruel wish in the heart."

"You and I may not be able always to tell the difference between a kind person and a selfish one," said Tang, "but there is One who is never fooled. That One always knows how we feel inside in our hearts."

When these Chinese travelers were back home again in their own country they never tired of talking about the Land-of-Great-Men. Each one would often wonder what the color of his own cloud would be if he had one. Sometimes they even talked to one another as if they had clouds, and naturally everyone began to want to keep his cloud bright like a rainbow.

The Whale and the Big Bronze Statue

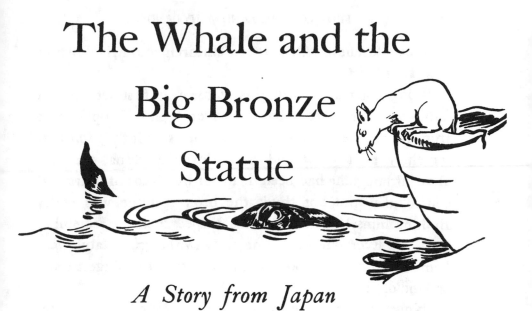

A Story from Japan

IN A LOVELY GARDEN not many miles from the city of
Yokohama in Japan there stands the tallest bronze statue
in the world. It was made to look like the man named
Buddha, who lived long ago in India. The Japanese who
planned this statue thought that the greatest man in the
world should have the biggest statue in the world.

This bronze Buddha, with his legs crossed under him,
is sitting upon an open lotus flower, also made of bronze.
The artist had the statue made in this way because when
Buddha taught he always sat with his legs crossed. The
lotus flower is there to remind us of something pure and
beautiful.

If you could stand beside this great statue, you would
have to hold your head way back and look up into the sky
to see his face—fifty feet above you. You could tuck yourself away in his ears—if you could ever climb up to them.
You could even sit on a drop of gold that sticks to the

Buddha's forehead. Or a dozen children could lie down in one of his hands.

Long, long ago when this statue was first set up and finished, it was talked about all over Japan. People came from far and near to see it. When they saw it they felt that somehow their great and much-loved Buddha was still alive, although he had been dead for hundreds of years. Of course, they did not think the bronze statue was really Buddha himself, but the statue helped them to remember Buddha. Everyone who came and saw the great statue went home to tell his neighbors that he had seen the biggest thing on land or sea.

Now, not far out in the vast ocean around Japan, there lived a great big Whale. Day after day he swam about wherever he wished, and every little while he spouted water from his great big snout, high in the air, with a proud swish. So big was this Whale that all the fishes in the ocean were afraid of him.

"What a wonderful animal I am!" thought the Whale. "I am the biggest thing in all the ocean. I must be bigger, too, than anything on the land." But one day a Shark swam up near the Whale and said:

"Mr. Whale, my lord, everybody is saying that a great statue has been set up in a park near Yokohama and that it is the biggest thing in all the world—on land or in the water!" On hearing this, the Whale roared angrily:

"How dare you say that there is something bigger than I?" He spouted so hard and roared so loudly that all the fishes darted away as fast as they could.

For many days the great big Whale sulked and pouted in an ugly way. He would not speak to any of the fishes.

It worried him to think there might be something bigger than he. He worried so much that he began to lose weight and to look old.

"This will never do," said he at last. "I am losing weight and I am growing weaker every day. I must find out for sure about that statue. I must know that I am still the biggest thing in all the world—on land or in the ocean." So the Whale called the Shark to him.

"Go and swim to the shore and find out for me if that statue of Buddha is really as big as people say it is."

Away swam the Shark. When he came near shore, he saw a boat lying near the beach. He swam up to it, hoping to find someone who could tell him about the big statue. As he looked about, he spied a Rat skipping across the deck. Softly the shark called: "Mr. Rat! Mr. Rat!"

"Who are you? What do you want?" came a sharp thin voice from the boat.

"Oh, Mr. Rat! My lord, the great big Whale in the ocean, has sent me to find out about that great big statue of Buddha that people say is not far from here."

"I know it well," said Mr. Rat. "It is very, very big."

"Would you then, dear Mr. Rat, do my lord, the great big Whale, a kindness and go to the statue and measure it? He simply must know how big it really is."

"Certainly, I shall be delighted to do so," said Mr. Rat, "if you will give me a couple of days' time to make the trip there and back."

So the next morning Mr. Rat hurried on his way. When he finally reached the park where the big statue stood he looked around to make sure nobody was watching. Then he walked all the way around the big statue counting his steps as he went. It took a long time for the Rat to walk all the way around. It took six thousand rat steps!

Mr. Rat then skipped back to the Shark who was waiting for him beside the boat near shore and reported that the statue was truly very, very big; so big, indeed, that it took him six thousand steps to go all around it. The Shark thanked his kind friend, Mr. Rat, and swam off to give the word to the great big Whale.

When the great big Whale heard that the statue was really and truly so big that it took six thousand steps for Mr. Rat to walk around it even once, the great big Whale tossed his snout high in the air and spouted angrily. "I won't believe it! I shall go and see that statue for myself."

So off the angry Whale swam. When he reached the shore he did a surprising thing. As quick as a wink, he turned his big tail into two magic feet, and off he walked, stepping like a giant across the fields and over the hills. In the middle of the night he finally arrived at the park where the statue stood. In the darkness the Whale could see only a great big blurred shadow towering before him.

"Good evening!" said the Whale in a deep voice.

"Good evening!" answered Buddha in a voice so great that the tall trees near by shook in fright. "Who are you? And where did you come from?"

"I am the great big Whale, the lord of all that swim in the ocean. I am the biggest animal on land or sea. But the Shark told me that you were bigger than I. So I made up my mind to come and see for myself. I cannot see in the dark how tall you are, but I shall wait here until morning, then I shall know."

As the light of the morning slowly turned the blurred

shadow into a clear shape, the great big Whale stood on his magic feet and stretched himself as high as he could. But no matter how hard he stretched there stood the great Buddha looking just as tall and big and round.

"I'm afraid the stories I have heard are true after all," sighed the great big Whale. "But I wish there were someone who could measure us both so that we might be sure which of us is the bigger."

Just then an old priest from the temple near by came up to the statue to kneel before it. When he saw the great big Whale standing on his two feet the priest was frightened almost out of his senses. He had never supposed anything else could be as big as the Buddha.

"Please," said the great big Whale and the great big

Buddha both at once, "please, measure us both to see which of us is really the taller."

So the old man took the scarf from his neck to use as a ruler. He ran for a ladder and set it up against the Whale's big body. He climbed up to the tip of the Whale's big snout and measured him from his head to his magic feet.

The priest then carried the ladder over to the bronze Buddha and laid it up against his body and measured it from top to bottom. All the while the great big Whale watched the old man very carefully to make sure that he was measuring fairly.

Finally, the priest told the great big Whale and the great big Buddha: "The Whale is just a wee bit taller. To be exact he is just six inches taller than the Buddha. That's not even as much as the length of one of Buddha's curls."

"Hurrah!" roared the great big Whale. "That settles it. I am the tallest and the longest thing on land or sea!"

Forgetting even to say "Thank you!" to the priest or "Good-by!" to Buddha, the great big Whale whirled about and ran with the steps of a giant across the fields and over the hills until he came to the ocean. Quick as a wink, he changed his two magic feet into a great big tail, and with a great big splash he slid into the water. Off he swam proudly into the middle of the ocean to tell all the fishes:

"After all I am really the biggest thing on land or sea."

As for the statue, it still stands in the grove of tall trees. Every year thousands of people travel from far and near to see it. They kneel before it and bring gifts of flowers to lay at its feet. But from that day to this the statue has never spoken. It sits without moving. It seems to stare out of its two golden eyes on all the people who come before it.

The Nervous
Little  Rabbit

A Story from India

ONCE UPON A TIME there was a nervous Little Rabbit. She was always afraid that something dreadful was going to happen to her. "Suppose the Sky were to fall down, what would happen to me then?" She said this so often that at last she really thought that some day the Sky would fall down.

"Or suppose the Earth were to fall in, what would happen to me then?" She said this also so often that at last she really thought that some day the Earth would fall in.

Once as she was running along under a coconut palm tree, she suddenly heard a noise. Something fell with a big thump. Little Rabbit was so frightened she could believe anything. "The Earth *is* falling in!" she cried as she ran away as fast as she could go.

Soon she met older Brother Rabbit. "Where are you going, Little Rabbit?" he asked.

Little Rabbit called: "The Earth is falling in and I am running away! I can't stop to tell you anything more."

"The Earth is falling in, is it?" said Brother Rabbit in surprise, but Little Rabbit kept running right along, and Brother Rabbit ran after her. Brother Rabbit soon met another rabbit and told him what Little Rabbit had said. This second rabbit ran along and soon told a third rabbit: "The Earth is falling in!" And the third rabbit told a fourth rabbit and so on and on the word was carried, until hundreds of rabbits were all shouting: "The Earth is falling in! The Earth is falling in!"

Soon some of the bigger animals heard the shouting, and they took up the cry. First Deer began calling: "The Earth is falling in!" Then Sheep, and then Wild Boar and then

Buffalo and then Camel and then Tiger and then Elephant trumpeted the cry: "The Earth is falling in!"

But when Lion heard all this shouting he insisted on knowing more about what had happened. "I see no signs that the Earth is falling in," he said. "These animals must have heard something."

Then Lion roared a call to all of the animals to stop their shouting. "What is this you are saying?" he asked.

Elephant replied: "I said that the Earth is falling in."

"How do you know this?" asked Lion.

"Why, now that I come to think about it, it was Tiger who told it to me."

And Tiger said: "I heard it from Camel." And Camel said: "I heard it from Buffalo." And Buffalo said: "I heard it from Wild Boar." And Wild Boar had heard it from Sheep. And Sheep had heard it from Deer, and Deer had heard it from one of the one hundred rabbits. And one of the rabbits said: "Oh, we heard it from that Little Rabbit."

Then Lion looked down on Little Rabbit and said: "Little Rabbit, what made you say that the Earth was falling in?"

"I saw it!" said Little Rabbit.

"You saw it?" asked Lion in surprise. "Where did you see it?"

"Over by that tree."

"Come with me," said Lion, "and show me just what happened."

"No, no, no," said Little Rabbit. "I would not go near that tree for anything in the world. I'm too afraid."

"I'm going to take you over on my back," said Lion, and he asked the other animals to wait until they returned.

So Lion carried Little Rabbit on his back over to the coconut palm tree. Lion said:

"Look up, Little Rabbit. What do you see growing on this tree?"

"I see some big round coconuts on the tree."

Just as Little Rabbit said this, a big round coconut fell off one of the branches on to the hard ground and made a big thump.

"What was it that made that big noise, Little Rabbit?"

"Oh, I see now! I see now!" cried Little Rabbit. "The Earth was not falling in at all. It must have been a big coconut like this one that dropped with a thump on the ground when I thought the Earth was falling in."

"Jump down off my back, Little Rabbit, and stand where I can look right at you. . . . Now," said Lion looking very solemn, "next time you hear a noise that frightens you, don't run away. Stop and look closely and see if you can find out just what has happened. Never guess when you can find out for yourself what is true."

"I'll remember! I'll remember!" said Little Rabbit very much impressed. "I have found out this time and I know the Earth is not falling in."

"Jump on my back again, Little Rabbit," said Lion. And he ran back with Little Rabbit through the woods to the place where the other animals were waiting for them.

This time when Little Rabbit told her story, the animals knew she was telling the truth. They were much relieved and began saying to each other: "The Earth is not falling in! The Earth is not falling in!"

One by one they scattered, each going toward his own part of the woods. As they ran, you could hear the words over and over: "The Earth is not falling in! The Earth is not falling in!"

But their calling grew softer and softer until once more all was quiet in the forest.

The Miller, His Boy and Their Donkey

A Story from Greece

A MILLER AND HIS BOY were once going with their Donkey to market. As they were walking along by its side a countryman passed them and said:

"You fools, what is a donkey for but to ride on?" So the Miller lifted his Boy up on the Donkey's back and they went on their way. But soon they passed a group of men, one of whom called:

"See that lazy youngster! He rides while he lets his father walk!" So the Miller ordered his Boy to get off, and he got on the Donkey himself. But they had not gone far when they passed two women.

"You lazy fellow!" called one of the women. "How can you have the heart to ride on your Donkey while your little Boy plods along scarcely able to keep up with you?"

So the good-natured Miller took his Boy up on the Donkey's back with him. By this time they had almost reached the town. Seeing two people on the back of a little

Donkey, the passers-by began to laugh and jeer and point fingers at them. The Miller stopped and asked: "What are you jeering at?" The answer came back:

"Lazybones, both of you! That poor old Donkey of yours can hardly walk. You and your big strong Boy ought to be ashamed of overloading him so."

"Anything to please you," said the good-natured Miller. So he and his Boy got down off the Donkey. The Miller found a stout pole, tied the Donkey's legs together with a rope and hung him to the pole. Then the Miller and his Boy lifted the ends of the pole on to their shoulders and off they started once more. This time they were carrying the Donkey.

Presently they came to a bridge over a river. Since the town was just across the river they met many people coming and going. When these people saw this strange sight, a Miller and a Boy carrying a Donkey, they laughed and laughed.

But the Donkey did not think the matter funny at all. He did not like being hung from a pole. He began kicking and squirming so hard that he soon got one foot free. In this way he knocked the pole off the Boy's shoulder. In the scuffle that followed the Donkey fell off the bridge into the river. Since his forefeet were still tied he could not swim and soon he was drowned. An old man who had been walking along the road behind the Miller and his Boy called out:

"That will teach you. If you try to please everybody you will please nobody, not even yourself."

The Wee, Wise Bird

A Story Told by Jewish Rabbis

LONG AGO IN A FARAWAY LAND a certain man took great pride in his beautiful garden. Each day he worked in some part of it, digging or planting, weeding or trimming the bushes. Each morning he strolled into all parts of his garden as if he wanted to encourage each little plant to keep on growing and to give a friendly smile to every bud that had opened into a flower.

One morning on taking his usual walk, the gardener noticed that leaves had been torn from some of his plants and that many of his flowers had been completely pecked to pieces. The gardener was puzzled and angry. He was determined to find out who had been destroying his garden.

The next morning he was again walking in the garden. He found more plants stripped of their leaves and more flowers torn into pieces. But this time he was prepared and he hid himself where he would not frighten any animal or bird that might be there.

As he waited, he was surprised to see a very small bird light upon a rosebud and peck it to pieces in almost no time at all. But the gardener, too, was quick. Before the wee bird had finished eating its second flower, he had it tight in his hand, and was carrying it off, intending to kill it. But strange to tell, the small bird began to talk to the gardener.

"Please, do not kill me, kind sir. I am only a small bird. If you cook me and eat me, I would give you only a mouthful—not one hundredth part of what a big man like you needs for a meal. I promise I will never come into your garden again. Please, let me go free. And what is more, I will teach you something that will be of great use to you and to your friends as long as you live."

The surprised gardener was in no mood to let this small bird get away from him. He talked back crossly.

"You may be a very small bird, but you are a very big nuisance. I will either make a quick end of you or you will make a quick end of my garden. I intend to kill you right now and eat you for supper. You are a bad little bird."

Even while the gardener was speaking so crossly, the wee bird felt soft and helpless in his hand. Its little heart beat so fast and so hard against his skin that he began to feel sorry for it. What is more, he began to be curious. What could this advice be that this wee bird wanted to give him? Would it really be useful to him. When the gardener again spoke, his voice was gentle.

"I am not a hateful or a cruel man, little bird. I am always glad to learn something new and useful. If from now on you will keep away from my garden, I *will* let you go free."

As soon as the wee bird promised, the gardener opened

his hand. But the bird did not fly away at once. Instead it stood right up straight in his open hand and again began talking.

"Listen, kind sir! Here are three rules for you to remember always. If you follow them, they will make your life easier and better. The first is this. *Never* cry for milk that has been spilt. Second, do not wish to have something that you know cannot be had. Third, do not believe what you know cannot possibly be true."

Having given the gardener these three wise rules, the wee bird lifted its wings and flew away and lighted upon the top branch of a near-by tree. From this high spot it began to call back with a sharp voice.

"What a silly man! The very idea of your letting me get away! If you only knew what you have lost! But it is too late now." Angrily the man called back:

"What have I lost?"

"Why, if you had killed me, as you intended, you would have found inside my body a beautiful pearl, as large as a goose's egg, and you could have sold that pearl and have been a rich man the rest of your life." The gardener, believing the little bird, thought to himself:

"What a fool I have been! I must persuade the bird to come back to me. I must have that big pearl."

"Dear little bird," he cried in his kindest voice, "sweet little bird, I will do you no harm if only you will come back to me. I will treat you as if you were my own child. I will give you fruit and flowers to eat every day. I promise you truly I will not kill you." But the wee bird shook its head and said firmly:

"What a silly man you are! How could you forget so

soon the advice which I gave you a few moments ago. I told you not to cry for spilt milk. And here you are crying over my being free. There is nothing now you can do about that just as you would gain nothing by crying over milk that had already been spilt on the floor.

"And besides I told you not to wish for what cannot be had. And now you are already wishing you could catch me again.

"And finally, I warned you against believing what you know cannot possibly be true, and yet you are thinking I told you the truth when I said a pearl was inside my body, as big as a goose's egg! You very well know that a goose's egg is larger than I am, and could not possibly be inside my body. You certainly are a silly and forgetful man. If you ever want to become wise you will have to remember your lessons better and longer than that."

With these words, the wee, wise bird lifted its small head in disgust and flew away. Although the foolish gardener never saw the bird again, he never forgot the advice it had given him.

Who Ate the Squabs?

A Story from Czechoslovakia

A SHOEMAKER'S WIFE baked two squabs, one for herself and one for her husband. When they were baked to a beautiful golden brown, she placed them in the small oven to keep them warm until time for dinner. She then went out to visit with a neighbor.

The shoemaker, meantime, kept sewing away on the shoe he was making. After a while he raised his head and sniffed the delicious smell that was coming from the oven. He began to feel hungry. Indeed, his wife was scarcely outside the gate, when he rose from his bench and walked over to the stove and reached his hand into the oven. He pulled out one of the squabs. "It looks so delicious," he thought, "I will just taste it." He cut off a small piece. But when he had once begun eating he wished for another taste and still another. Before long the whole squab was eaten up. "I'll just tell my wife I couldn't wait," he thought. "She will forgive me."

He sat down again beside his bench and took up the shoe on which he had been working. But he was still hungry. He knew there was another squab in the oven. Again he rose from his bench, and walked over to the oven. He pulled out the second squab. He ate this even more quickly than he had eaten the first one.

When he had finished and saw the bones lying on the table, he began to be a little worried. He gathered up the bones and carried them outside into the yard and buried them.

He sat down once more on his workbench and began sewing fast and hard. He felt pleased with himself and yet he began to be troubled. What could he say to his wife now? How could she forgive him? He was disgusted with himself for being so greedy. He would feel like a pig if he told her the truth. He was almost on the point of running away and never coming back. But he couldn't make up his mind.

About noon his wife came home and started to prepare the dinner. When everything else was ready, she went to the oven to look at her squabs.

"Who ate the squabs?" she shouted, slamming the oven door shut.

"Don't ask me. I didn't," came the shoemaker's grumbling voice. "Over here at my bench I didn't even notice that you had been baking anything."

"Who else has been here? Who else could have eaten them?"

"I was out for a while this morning. Someone might have come in and taken them off."

"None of our neighbors would ever do a thing like

that. And you know it very well. You ate those squabs and you are afraid to say so."

"You must have taken the squabs with you, woman, when you went out. You ate them yourself where I couldn't see you."

"I did not!" shouted his angry wife.

"Well, don't be asking me about them. I've been too busy here at my bench all morning to stop and eat two squabs."

So the arguing went back and forth, back and forth. Of course, the wife would not say she had eaten the squabs when she hadn't, and the shoemaker was ashamed to admit what he had done. Finally the wife said:

"Well, let's not quarrel any longer. Let's not talk to each other at all. I will say nothing. You will say nothing. When being silent becomes unbearable, the first one to speak will be the guilty one."

So the matter was left as the wife suggested. For the rest of the day and evening, neither one of them said a single word. The wife could not gossip about the people she had seen in the market. The shoemaker could not ask for anything of his wife. The wife could not complain. The shoemaker could not sing at his work. The quietness was very annoying, but neither one would speak first.

Three long and tiresome days and nights of silence passed by. Finally on the fourth morning a gentleman with horse and carriage drove up to the shoemaker's gate. His coachman jumped down from the carriage and knocked at the door. The wife went to the door and opened her mouth to say "Good morning!" but she quickly remembered and shut it before she had spoken. The stranger asked the road to take to reach the city. The wife merely pointed with her hand to show the direction.

The servant ran back to the carriage to tell his master that there were two dumb people in the house who could not talk. This was more than the wife could bear. She ran out to the carriage, and climbed up on the seat beside the gentleman. With her hands she made known to him that she would go along and show them the way. The gentleman shoved over on the seat and made room for her. The coachman touched his horse with his whip, and the carriage started off.

By this time the shoemaker was really frightened. He thought his wife was going to leave him for good. This he could not let her do. He shouted from the doorway:

"Wife, little wife! Do not go away from me! Please forgive me! I did eat those squabs!"

His wife jumped right out of the carriage and the shoemaker ran out the door. He threw his arms around her and kissed her, and they both burst out laughing. It was such a relief after having their hurt and angry feelings all shut up inside them for three whole days.

They told the whole story to the gentleman in the carriage and he and his coachman chuckled all the way to the city.

The
Two
Cheats

A Story from Uganda

EVERYBODY LIKES GOOD THINGS to eat, and pretty cloth to make dresses out of, but we are not all agreed on what kind of cloth is the prettiest, or which kinds of food taste the best.

In Uganda the people used to like cloth that was made out of pieces of bark, pounded thin and colored with interesting patterns. As for a real bit of tasty food, nothing seemed better than big fried ants with their white wings cut off. In Uganda these ants grow very large, and when fried, they taste somewhat like shrimp. These big ants can be gotten only twice a year—when the rains begin. Like certain other things that are scarce, these fried ants have seemed especially delicious to the people of Uganda.

Once upon a time there were two merchants. One bought and sold bark cloth and the other gathered ants and prepared them for sale by frying them. One of the merchants lived in one village and the other lived in another village. The two men had never seen each other.

One day the man who sold bark cloth thought he would play a trick and earn a little extra money. So he collected a lot of useless rags and pieces of soft bark rubbish and gathered them into a neat roll. On the outside he wrapped a couple of layers of beautiful bark cloth and tied the bundle with some pretty bark-cloth ribbon. The bundle looked like a big roll of yards and yards of beautiful bark cloth.

Very much pleased with himself, the man put the bundle on his shoulder and walked off toward the village of Kijongo where he planned to sell the bundle in the market place.

Now the other merchant from the other village also thought of a trick he would play and so make some extra money. He had a great many more ants' wings, which were good for nothing, than he had fried ants. So he, too, made a pretty looking bundle all wrapped in clean strong banana leaves. But inside the bundle he put a lot of useless ants' wings, and covered them with a layer of banana leaves; and then he put a layer of big fried ants just underneath the outer cover.

Very much pleased with himself, the man put the bundle on his shoulder and walked off toward the village of Kijongo where he planned to sell the bundle in the market place.

There in the market place, the two men sat, one opposite the other on the street. Opening his bundle part way, the first merchant called:

"Who will buy this lovely roll of bark cloth?" Opening

his bundle part way, the second merchant spread some big fried ants out on a banana leaf.

"Who wants to buy some delicious fried ants?" he called.

Finally when the market day was nearly over and neither man had sold his bundle, the merchant with the bark cloth was tired and hungry. He said to the man with the fried ants:

"I do not wish to buy your fried ants but I will exchange them for my roll of bark cloth. That surely is a big bargain for you. I shouldn't think of offering this big roll of bark cloth for such a small bundle of fried ants, but I am almost dying of hunger." The man with the fried ants thought to himself:

"I would really be getting a wonderful bargain. Think of it—a big roll of beautiful bark cloth for a few fried ants!" So he agreed to the exchange.

Each man tried to hide his secret pleasure over the bargain he had made. Without more words each shouldered his new bundle, and started off for his own village, very much pleased with himself.

But imagine their surprise when they opened their bundles! The people of Uganda have never forgotten the two cheats. Now, whenever anyone in the country tries to cheat, the people say:

"Remember the two cheats that met at the Kijongo market."

The
Old
Bowl

A Story from India

ONCE IN THE LONG AGO in India, two men with heavy bundles of pots and bowls hung over their shoulders entered a certain town to sell their wares. In fairness to each other, they had agreed to divide the streets of the town between them. Each was to sell only in his half of the town until after the other had completed his rounds.

In one of the old houses in this town there lived a young girl and her grandmother. Once their family had been large and rich, but now only the two of them were left and they were very poor. Most of the beautiful things they used to have in the house had been sold to buy food and clothes. But there was one old bowl that the grandmother had kept because her father had used it for so many years. It lay among the pots and pans on one of the kitchen shelves, almost forgotten and so covered with dirt that it looked like an ordinary brass bowl.

Presently one of the peddlers came walking down the

street. He rang his bell as over and over he sang his song:

"Beautiful pots and pans for sale! Everything you want in brass or tin!" He stopped at the door of the old woman's house. Her granddaughter looked longingly at the bright and shining things dangling from the peddler's shoulders. She invited him in and offered him a chair:

"Please, grandmother, buy something pretty for me."

"We are too poor, my child. What can we possibly give the man in exchange for even a small thing?"

The girl would not give up. She ran to the kitchen and looked among the pots and pans. She brought out the dirty little old bowl.

"Here's this old bowl, grandmother, that we never, never use. May I give it to the peddler?" The old woman thought she might as well let the young girl have her way.

"Will you give our little sister some small thing in exchange for this old bowl?" she asked.

The peddler took the bowl in his hands and felt of it. He turned it over and with a needle scratched a thin line on the bottom of the bowl. To his surprise he found there was gold underneath the dirt. But he did not say a word. He made his face look as if he thought the bowl was simply made of brass. He thought to himself: "Perhaps I can get a very valuable bowl without paying anything for it." But aloud he said:

"This old bowl isn't worth even a halfpenny." He threw it on the floor as if in disgust and walked out the door.

Now the two peddlers had agreed that it would be fair for either of them to go down a street in the half of the town that had been given to the other provided he waited until after the first peddler had been there. So after a time the second peddler, whose name was Seriva, came walking down the street. He rang his bell as over and over he sang his song:

"Beautiful pots and pans for sale! Everything you want in brass or tin." As he passed this very same house the young girl called:

"Please, grandmother, buy something pretty for me. Let me ask this peddler if he will take our old bowl in exchange for something new."

"My child," said the grandmother, "the other peddler threw the bowl on the floor. He said it was not worth bothering with. We have nothing else to give."

"But, grandmother, that peddler was a cross old man. This one looks pleasant. I like the sound of his voice. He might take the bowl."

"Call the peddler in, my child."

So the young girl called the peddler in and gave him a chair. Then she asked him timidly: "What will you give us for this bowl? I want some little pretty thing."

Seriva took the bowl in his hands. He turned it over and with a needle he scratched a thin line on the bottom.

"Lady," he said in surprise, "this is a golden bowl! It is worth a thousand silver pieces! All the things I have with me would not be enough to give you in exchange for this!"

"But, sir," said the old woman, "another peddler just came by. He threw the old bowl on the floor in disgust and said it wasn't worth a halfpenny. You must be mistaken or else the bowl has changed to gold in your hands. Sir, we will make you a present of it. Just give us some trifle for it in return. I don't like to disappoint my granddaughter."

Then the peddler gave the old woman all the brass and tinware in his bundles. He gave her also five hundred pieces of silver. He kept only eight pennies out of all the money he had, just enough to pay the boatman on the river to paddle him across the river and home. With the golden bowl in his hand, he ran singing down the street and off to the river's bank.

There he found the boatman, gave him the eight pennies, jumped into the boat and off he went.

Just a few moments later, the first peddler was back on the street again and knocked at the old woman's door.

"I've decided to give you a little something for that old bowl of yours," he said. "I know how eager your little girl is for something pretty."

"You greedy man!" shouted the old woman. "You said the old bowl was not worth a halfpenny and you knew all the time it was solid gold. Another peddler has just been here. He has given me everything he had for the bowl. He said it was worth a thousand pieces of silver."

"A thousand pieces of silver!" cried the angry peddler. "A thousand pieces of silver! And I have lost them all!

"I'll catch the old sneak. I'll catch him yet. I'll make him divide his gold!" The peddler was so mad he did not know what he was doing. He rushed so fast out the door that he did not know he had dropped his own moneybag. He did not hear the sound of his pots and pans crashing to the floor.

When he reached the riverbank, he saw the other peddler far out in the river. "Stop! Come back!" he shouted.

"Don't stop!" said Seriva to the boatman, and the angry

peddler was left standing on the bank to kick and shout helplessly until he wore himself out.

But the honest peddler had an exciting story to tell his family when he reached home. The next day he sold the old bowl for even more money than he had paid for it. With the extra money, Seriva's wife was able to buy new cloth and make new clothes for her children. And Seriva took great delight in being able now and then to give small gifts to his friends, especially to those who never before in their lives had ever had a pretty thing all their own.

Human Diversity

The Blind Men
and the Elephant

A Story from India

LONG, LONG AGO in India a company of men lived together by themselves in a large house outside the town.
Every day some of them would go into the town with empty
cups in their hands and beg for money with which to buy
food. Much of the rest of the time the men spent quietly
thinking and talking together. The questions they tried to
answer were always very hard questions, such as these:
"Does a person live again after he dies?" or "What is God
like?"

Different men gave different answers to these questions,
and each one was sure his answer was right. "I'm right and
you're wrong," one man would say. "No, you're wrong and
I'm right," the other would insist. Sometimes these men
became so excited over their differences that they would
quarrel and wrangle loudly with one another. Sometimes
their tongues seemed sharp as daggers.

Finally one morning these monks, as they were called,
went to their most honored teacher, Buddha. They asked

him to help them and to decide which one was right and which one was wrong. Buddha answered them by telling this story:

Once there was a certain King who gave this order to his servant: "Go, young man, and gather together in one place all the men in the town who were born blind."

When the blind men had all come together, the King said to his servant: "Now bring me an elephant."

When the elephant had been brought, the King said to the blind men: "Standing before you now is what we call an elephant. Each one of you may touch this elephant, and when you have done so I want you to tell me what an elephant is like."

So the servant led the blind men one by one close to the elephant. He let the first blind man feel the elephant's head. He let the second blind man feel the elephant's ears. He let the third blind man feel the elephant's tusks. He let the fourth man feel the elephant's trunk. He let the fifth man feel the elephant's legs. He let the sixth man feel the elephant's back. And he let the last blind man feel the elephant's tail.

When each blind man had felt the elephant, the King asked them: "Now tell me, one by one, what an elephant is like." The blind man who had felt the elephant's head said:

"Your Majesty, an elephant is like a large waterpot." The blind man who had felt the elephant's ears said:

"Your Majesty, he is wrong. An elephant is like a flat basket." The blind man who had felt the elephant's tusk said:

"Your Majesty, they are both wrong. An elephant is

like the sharp end of a plow." The blind man who had felt
the elephant's trunk said:

"Your Majesty, they are all wrong. An elephant is like
a thick rope." The blind man who had felt the elephant's
back and body said:

"Your Majesty, that man is also wrong. An elephant is
like a big crib full of wheat." The blind man who had felt
the elephant's legs said:

"Your Majesty, all of these men are wrong. An elephant is like four pillars." The blind man who had felt the
elephant's tail said:

"Your Majesty, I am the only one who knows. An elephant is like a fan."

When they had all finished telling what they thought
an elephant was like, they began to argue. One shouted:
"An elephant is like a crib full of wheat!" Another shouted:
"No, I tell you, an elephant is like the sharp point of a
plow!" And so they argued on and on until the King had
to command them to be quiet.

When Buddha had finished this story he turned to the
quarreling men sitting in front of him and said: "How can
you be so sure of what you cannot see? We are all like blind
men in this world. We cannot see God. Nor can we know
what is going to happen after we die. Each one of you may
be partly right in your answers. Yet none of you is fully
right. Let us not quarrel over what we cannot be sure of."

So the quarreling and the wrangling stopped. Yet the
men still kept on wondering and talking over their thoughts.
They realized that they were asking questions that no one
has ever fully answered.

A Ring-around of Temper

A Story from Burma

ONCE UPON A TIME there was a man by the name of Chem who lived in the country of Burma. He was standing by his hut on the bank of a river, sharpening his ax when a little shrimp crawled up on his foot and bit him.

Chem became so angry that he lifted his ax and cut a near-by tree with a fierce blow.

The tree became so angry that it shook a coconut as big as a melon from one of its branches, and the coconut fell on the back of a rooster.

The rooster became so angry that he scratched up a big anthill, full of hundreds of ants.

The ants became so angry that they crawled off and bit the tail of a snake.

The snake became so angry that he stung a wild pig in the leg.

The wild pig became so angry that he dug his snout

into the root of a plantain tree, and a bat that was sleeping in a branch of the tree tumbled to the ground.

The bat became so angry that he flew into the ear of an elephant.

The elephant became so angry that he knocked over a big round hollow stone on which an old woman used to pound her rice. The stone rolled down the hill and hit the old woman's house and knocked it down.

"Stone! Stone!" called the old woman angrily. "You must pay me for my house."

"I won't! I won't!" shouted the stone. "It was the elephant who made me roll down the hill."

The old woman went to the elephant, and said angrily: "Elephant, you must pay me for my house."

"No, I won't!" said the elephant. "It was the bat's fault. He flew into my ear." The old woman went to the bat and said angrily:

"Bat, you must pay me for my house."

"No, I won't!" said the bat. "It was the wild pig's fault. He uprooted the tree where I was sleeping." The old woman went to the wild pig and said angrily:

"Pig, you must pay me for my house."

"No, I won't!" said the wild pig. "It was the snake's fault. He stung me in the leg." The old woman went to the snake and said angrily:

"Snake, you must pay me for my house."

"No, I won't!" said the snake. "It was the fault of the ants. They bit my tail." The old woman went to the ants and said angrily:

"Ants, you must pay me for my house."

"No, we won't!" said the ants. "It was the rooster's

fault. He scratched up our hill and spoiled our house."
The old woman went to the rooster and said angrily:

"Rooster, you must pay me for my house."

"No, I won't!" said the rooster. "It was the coconut
tree's fault. It dropped a coconut on my back." The old
woman went to the coconut tree, and said angrily:

"Coconut tree, you must pay me for my house."

"No, I won't!" said the coconut tree. "It was that man
Chem who struck me with his ax." The old woman went
to Chem and said angrily:

"Chem, you must pay me for my house."

"No, I won't!" said Chem. "It's the fault of the shrimp.
He bit my foot." The old woman went to the little shrimp
and said:

"Shrimp, you must pay me for my house."

Now the shrimp could not blame anyone else. Nor
could he build the old woman a new house.

While she was scolding him, the shrimp hopped into a
pool, dived down to the bottom, and no one has ever been
able to find him since.

The Blind Man
and
the
Lame Man

A Story from Uganda

THE MEN OF THE VILLAGE of Gomba were fighting with the men of another village, and nobody in Gomba was safe. Two men in the village were especially frightened because they were almost completely forgotten by everyone else. One was a lame man and the other was a blind man.

Every morning the lame man was carried by his son out into the open courtyard and each evening he was carried back into the house. But all day long he sat, and few there were who even stopped to talk with him.

One day as he sat alone and forgotten, he saw the blind man down the street groping his way along with a stick. Men with spears in their hands ran past him and pushed him aside, as if he were rubbish, and knocked him to the ground. Suddenly the lame man had a thought. He called to the blind man:

"Come here, my friend, I have something important to tell you." When the blind man heard the friendly call, he lifted himself up and groped his way in the direction of the lame man, until at last he stood in front of him.

"Listen, my friend," said the lame man. "No one has remembered either of us during this fighting. We shall surely die if we stay here."

"You have spoken the truth," said the blind man. "I thought a moment ago that I was going to be trampled on. It's a wonder I got away with no bones broken."

"We must find a way to escape to another village where there is no fighting," said the lame man. "I have a plan. You are blind and I am lame. Take me on your back and I shall be eyes to you and you shall be feet to me."

Since the plan seemed very good, the blind man hoisted the lame man on his back, and the lame man showed him the way to go. At last they reached another village where the men were not fighting and the two men once more felt safe. When the blind man had set the lame man on the ground, he said: "Surely you will give me some reward for carrying you on my back, for I have saved your life." But the lame man answered:

"Not so. It was I who saved your life." So the two men argued. They spoke hot and angry words to each other.

At last they decided to take their case to the chief of the village. When he heard their story he said: "You should call it quits. The lame man was eyes to the blind man and the blind man was feet to the lame man. Each of you saved his own life. What greater reward can you wish?"

So it has become a proverb in Uganda. When two men quarrel and both of them are partly in the right or both of them are partly in the wrong, the people say:

"It is a case of the Quits of Gomba."

The Two Friends

A Story from India

L ONG AGO THE KING of Benares had a beautiful white Elephant that he loved to ride. The King's servants were commanded to give her the best of care. Each day they led the Elephant out of her stable and into a green field where she might eat grass freely. Once a day her keeper brought her to a deep, clear pool where she might splash and play as much as she wanted, and regularly he brought large pots of rice into her stall for her to eat.

One day while the Elephant was enjoying her midday meal a stray Dog wandered into the stables and to the Elephant's side. There the Dog began feeding on the small lumps of rice that fell at the Elephant's feet. So pleasant was this experience that the Dog returned again and again to eat alongside the big white Elephant. Soon the two animals became friends. After their meals they would play together. The Dog would jump up and sit on the Elephant's trunk, and the Elephant would swing the little Dog back and forth. To swing on an Elephant's trunk was a jolly game for a Dog. And to have a happy Dog to swing on her trunk was lots of fun for a big Elephant. Soon the two were very close friends. If for any reason the Dog did not come for a meal, the Elephant began to worry. She was unhappy until the Dog appeared again.

After some time a farmer from another village came to the stable and saw the Dog playing with the Elephant. At once the farmer wished that the Dog might be his. He offered to buy it from the Elephant keeper. So the keeper sold the Dog to the farmer for a good price, and the farmer took the Dog back home with him.

That night when the Dog did not come to lie down to sleep beside the Elephant she began to worry. When the next morning passed and still the Dog did not come the Elephant felt so sad she refused to eat her rice. The next morning she would not eat the grass in the fields. And the following morning the keeper could not even pull her off

to the pool for a swim. Day after day went by. The Elephant seemed to care for nothing at all. She would not eat. She would not bathe.

Finally, the keeper sent word to the King that his favorite Elephant would neither eat nor bathe. What should he do? The King called Bodisat, his chief adviser.

"Go, sir," said the King, "to the stables and find out what the matter is with my favorite Elephant."

Bodisat went and looked the Elephant over from head to foot. He could find nothing wrong anywhere at all. He turned to the Elephant keeper and said:

"There is nothing wrong anywhere with the Elephant's body. But there is something wrong with her feelings. She seems to me to be sorrowing over something. I wonder if she is lonely for someone. Is there another animal with whom she used to play who has been taken away?"

"Yes," said the Elephant keeper. "There was a stray Dog that used to come here every mealtime and eat of the small lumps of rice that fell at the Elephant's feet. The two of them used to play together every day."

"Where is the Dog now?" asked Bodisat.

"A man came one day and took the Dog away."

"Do you know where the man lives?"

"No, sir, I do not." Bodisat then returned to the King and told him:

"There is nothing the matter with the Elephant's body, your Majesty. Her trouble is in her feelings. That Elephant had a Dog friend, I am told, who used to come at mealtimes and play with her, and someone has taken the Dog away."

On hearing this, the King made a proclamation and

commanded that it be made known in all the villages of his kingdom.

"Some man has taken away a Dog who was a friend of my favorite white Elephant. That man in whose house the Dog is found will have to pay a fine if he does not return the animal at once."

As soon as the farmer in his far-off village heard of the King's proclamation, he was frightened and he let the Dog loose. Of its own accord it ran all the way back to the Elephant's stable and rubbed its nose against the Elephant's legs. As soon as the big white Elephant spied her old friend she lowered her trunk. Up jumped the happy Dog. The Elephant curled up her trunk with the Dog on it and placed him right on top of her forehead. Then she trumpeted with a happy trumpet call that was heard all the way to the King's palace.

Soon the big white Elephant let the Dog slide right down her trunk onto the floor. She watched him as he ate greedily of the lumps of rice scattered at her feet. Then the big white Elephant began eating also, and once more all was happiness in the big white Elephant's house. And never again as long as they lived were the Elephant and her friend the Dog far apart.

The King never forgot Bodisat, his wise adviser, who knew how to cure an animal's sick feelings.

King Saul Finds a Harpist

A Story from Palestine

K ING SAUL WAS HIS country's first King. He was a handsome, tall man who stood head and shoulders above everyone else. Before being made King, Saul had been a fighter and a bold leader of other fighters.

King Saul's people were newcomers in the country of Canaan. They had grown tired of living on desert land where they could do nothing but hunt and raise sheep. So for some years these Hebrews had been moving into this better country of Canaan. They had been coming—hundreds of them at a time.

But the Canaanites had been living in this country of Canaan for many hundreds of years. They thought the land belonged to them. They did not want these newcomers. Even though some of the new people settled down quietly on the hillsides outside the Canaanite towns, the Canaanites did not like these foreigners at all.

So fighting began between the Hebrews and the Canaanites. Many on both sides were killed. By the time this story begins, the newcomers had taken over many miles of country. They had driven thousands of the Canaanites out of their own towns; they had pushed them off their own farm lands, and had forced them to go far away to build new homes for themselves.

Being a King in a little country that had never before had a King was not at all easy. But it was still harder when the people who had been living there before thought their country had been wrongfully stolen from them.

Perhaps having to live in a fortress with armed soldiers around everywhere all the time made King Saul nervous. Or, perhaps hearing stories of fighting and killing day after day was more than he could stand. At any rate, before long King Saul became a sick and discouraged man. Spells would come on him when he did not seem to know what he was doing. King Saul's family became frightened and could not think what to do for him.

Finally, someone suggested that a young man be found who could play on the harp, and that he be brought to the palace to live so that, whenever the King felt one of his sick spells coming upon him, the boy might be called to play pleasant and quieting music for the King. On hearing of this plan someone at court said:

"I know just the young man for the King. His name is David and he is a shepherd boy who lives near Bethlehem. He plays the harp beautifully."

So David, the shepherd boy, was sent for, and he came to the palace and became one of the King's servants. Immediately he was taken notice of because of his handsome face and his friendly way. King Saul loved to sit and listen

to the music David's fingers could bring out of his harp.
Whenever the King felt a sick spell coming David would
be quickly called. As the sweet tones rippled through the
room the King would slowly become calm again, and by the
time the music was ended he would be feeling much better.

Young David was given a room in the palace. He ate
at the royal table with the King, his two princes and the
nobles of the court. Every day David saw and talked with
King Saul's two beautiful daughters, Merah and Michal.
He was so friendly with everyone and so careful to do just
as the King wished, that soon the King felt his new harpist
was just like one of the family. He really began to love
David as if he were one of his own sons. In fact David be-

came a favorite with the whole family. Jonathan, the King's oldest son, was especially fond of him. They played together, talked together, and went hunting together. Sometimes they even went together to fight the Canaanites.

Before long both David and Jonathan were made captains in King Saul's army. As a leader of soldiers, David was just as popular as he was as a harpist in King Saul's palace. They liked him because they found he was always ready to face danger. Perhaps his men had heard the stories of how, when he was a shepherd, he had fought singlehanded and had killed both a lion and a bear. Many also knew the story of how, armed merely with a stone and a sling, he had fought a giant and killed him.

Whenever the people saw David and his army marching back into the royal city they lined the streets and shouted and sang. Larger crowds used to gather when David and his men returned from fighting than when Jonathan and his men came back. They even shouted and sang more loudly for David than they did for King Saul himself.

Little by little the King began to notice David's greater popularity and he began to be jealous. "If this continues, David will soon be King instead of me" he thought. So King Saul kept close watch on the young man.

In the meantime King Saul's younger daughter Michal had fallen in love with the popular harpist and warrior. When the King learned of this, he was pleased, for he thought to himself: "If Michal becomes David's wife she can spy upon him and thus protect the family."

So King Saul sent word to David: "The King is pleased with you. All the royal household is pleased. My daughter Michal loves you. Will you become my son-in-law?"

David was glad when he received the King's message, for he was very much in love with Michal. The wedding was celebrated in the palace with much feasting and dancing. The King's household and all the people were excited and happy. But King Saul was not happy. In his heart he was jealous and afraid. Finally, one day he secretly called Jonathan to him:

"You must find a way to have David killed. As long as he lives you will never become king of this country." Jonathan protested.

"Father, David has done nothing wrong. Indeed his conduct has been exceedingly good toward you always. Again and again he has risked his life for your sake. Why then will you do wrong and take the life of an innocent man?"

Jonathan pleaded so well for his friend David that the King was quieted for a time. Jonathan was comforted and went to David and assured him that his father was no longer jealous. Soon David was again going in and out of the palace just as freely as in the beginning, and for a while all seemed to be going well.

Unfortunately King Saul's jealousy once more began to grow until one day he had an exceptionally bad spell of madness. David was called. He began playing his harp with all his usual charm; but, alas, it seemed as though King Saul could not even hear the music. Instead of calming down, he grew more and more restless until he became violently mad. He reached for his spear and threw it at David. Fortunately, David jumped quickly just in time and ran out of the room. With the help of friends, he hid until it was dark and then he escaped into the country.

David and Jonathan Become Friends

A Story from Palestine

IN THE DARKNESS DAVID went to find his friend Jonathan.

"What have I done, Jonathan?" he asked. "What is my guilt? Why is your father trying to take my life?"

"Put the idea out of your thoughts, David. You shall not die. I will protect you. My father does nothing either great or small but he tells it to me. Why should he be hiding anything from me now? It cannot be so."

"Yes, it is so, Jonathan," said David. "Your father well knows that you are fond of me and he is saying: 'Do not let Jonathan know this, for he will feel badly.' Yet, Jonathan, as sure as you live and as sure as I live, there is but one step between me and death."

"What do you want me to do, David?"

"This is my plan, Jonathan. Tomorrow is the festival of the new moon. I shall not come to the palace to sit down at the King's table. Instead I shall go and hide myself somewhere in the country. If your father misses me and asks about me, you must say: 'David urgently asked me to give him leave to go home to Bethlehem for this festival. His family are begging him and it has been a long time since he was with them.' If your father says: 'Good,' then all is well with me. But if he becomes angry, then you will know that he is determined to kill me. Make a promise to me, Jonathan. If I have done wrong, kill me yourself. Don't make me go back to your father again."

"David, if I find my father is determined to kill you, I promise I will tell you plainly."

"But how can you let me know if your father answers you harshly?" asked David.

"Come, let us both go together into the open country where we can be alone," said Jonathan. So in the early dawn before the city had awakened, these two walked together out toward the hills. For a long while neither one said a word. Finally Jonathan began solemnly:

"Let God himself hear what I am going to say to you, David. You will be missed at the King's table, but my father may not say anything the first day or even the second. By the third day he will surely ask me about you. The morning after that I will come out here to this place. You will be sitting over there behind that heap of stones. I will shoot several arrows in that general direction as if I were shooting at something. Then I will send my boy to pick up the arrows. If I say to him: 'See, the arrows are on this side of you! Go there and pick them up!' then, David, you may come out of hiding, for you will know that all is well. But if I say to the boy: 'See, the arrows are beyond you!' you will know you must escape. Your life is in danger."

The two solemnly agreed to the plan and David promised to keep in hiding until the time when Jonathan would come.

The great feast of the new moon was prepared in the palace. King Saul and all his family and noblemen sat down to eat, but David's place was empty. The King said nothing, however, the first day, for he thought:

"There has perhaps been some little accident to delay his coming." But on the second day, when he found David's place still empty, the King said to Jonathan:

"Why has not David come to the feast, either yesterday or today?"

"Father, David asked leave of me to go to Bethlehem yesterday. He wanted to observe the festival with his family. His brothers have been begging him to come home. This is why he has not come to the King's table." King Saul stiffened with anger. His words exploded from his mouth like fire .

"The way you are associating with this son of a country farmer is a shame to yourself and to your mother. As long as that scoundrel lives you will never be King. Go and bring David to me at once, for he must die."

"Why should he be put to death?" shouted Jonathan hotly. "What evil has he done?"

Quickly King Saul reached for his spear and lifted it to throw even at his own son Jonathan to kill him.

But Jonathan rose from the table in hot anger. He would eat no more. He ran out of the hall and away from the palace. He knew now that David was right. The King was determined on his death. Jonathan then felt hurt by his father's attitude, and felt distressed because of his friend.

In the morning, as he had promised, Jonathan set out with his bow and arrows as if to hunt, and a small boy went with him. When they reached the hillside where he and David had agreed to meet, Jonathan shot several arrows in the direction of the pile of rocks behind which he knew his friend was hiding.

"Run and pick up the arrows!" Jonathan called to the boy. As the boy ran toward the rocks, Jonathan called again:

"Are not the arrows farther ahead beyond you? Hurry, quick, do not stop!"

So the boy gathered up the arrows and brought them to his master. But Jonathan handed them back to the boy, together with his bow, saying:

"Go back now to the city. I am staying on here for a while alone."

As soon as the boy was well out of sight, David came out of hiding from behind the heap of stones, and ran to Jonathan. He fell down on his knees before his friend, but Jonathan lifted David up and kissed him, for he loved David with all his heart. For a long time neither one could say a word. They simply wept on each other's shoulders. Finally Jonathan spoke:

"David, you are dearer to me than a brother. But now you must go. I promise you that I and my children and our children's children shall be friends of yours forever." And David promised the same to Jonathan.

So the two friends parted. Jonathan returned to his father's palace. David walked off alone in the opposite direction toward the woods.

The King's Spear and Water Jug

A Story from Palestine

IT DID NOT TAKE LONG for the rumor to spread that David was in hiding somewhere in the mountains south of King Saul's city and that his life was in danger. At once, his friends began to hunt for him in order to help him. People who were in trouble themselves came and joined his company. Many came who felt bitter because of the way they themselves had been treated. All sorts of discontented and unhappy people came. They knew that David would be their friend and they wanted to be his friends. They had decided that they would rather fight to protect David than fight for King Saul. Before long as many as four hundred men were in hiding with David.

It was a hard life for them all. Like the wild animals around them on the mountains, they rested quietly during the daytime in some cave or in the thick shadows of the forest, and during the dark hours of the night they would often move on to a new hiding place.

The King had spies everywhere trying to find out where the outlaws were. If some stranger caught sight of them, word was almost sure to be carried back to the King. So they were constantly on their guard.

One day, it is said, Jonathan heard of David's place of hiding and, without letting anyone in the palace know, he slipped away in the hope of having a few words with his friend.

When the two actually met in the shadows of the forest, there was not time to say much and it was hard for them to put their feelings into words at all. Jonathan did most of what talking was done. David could never forget his parting words.

"Heart of my heart, keep up your courage. Don't let yourself be afraid. I know that some day you are going to be the King. When that time comes, all I want is to be next to you, David, and to help you. Remember, we are friends forever."

Again they kissed each other. Their eyes were wet with tears as they parted. Some time later a certain man went to King Saul and said:

"We know just the mountain where David and his men are now hiding."

At once King Saul, with a large company of soldiers, started out, determined to find David and to kill him. But in the meantime, a friend sent a messenger secretly to David, warning him of the King's coming. David quickly moved and made camp on top of a mountain on the other side of the valley from where he had been.

In the dusk of evening David looked down from the high cliff on which he and his men were camped. He saw

a campfire low on the hill on the opposite side of the valley. He said to his companions:

"Who will go down with me tonight into the King's
camp?"

"I will," said Abishai, David's young nephew.

Several hours later in the darkness of a starry night,
David and Abishai climbed down the mountainside and
walked across the valley and up the hill toward the King's
camp. All was dark and still except for the low flickering
of the campfire. Sleeping men were lying around on the
ground everywhere. Abishai whispered:

"Uncle David, we now have the King in our hands. Let
me steal quietly up to him and pin him to the earth with
his own spear. I promise it will take but one stroke. His
soldiers will never fight as soon as they know you are here."
But David said to his young nephew:

"No, Abishai. Let us not be the ones to kill our King.
His day to die will come. But I will do this, Abishai: I
will make my way quietly over to where the King lies
asleep and I will steal something of his and come back to
you. Then let both of us get away as fast and as quietly as
we can."

With footsteps soft as those of a lion in the forest, David
moved in between the sleeping men on the ground. With
each step he feared that someone would awaken, but not a
person stirred. David began wondering, as he looked into
face after face, whether he would recognize the King if he
saw him. And suppose he were to come upon his old enemy,
could he resist the urge to kill him? Why, after all,
shouldn't he kill the man who was out to kill him? If Saul
were dead, he, David, might be King! David's heart

pounded fast as he stepped between the sleeping bodies. His feelings were not as quiet as his footsteps.

At last David found the King, lying sound asleep on the ground, a little apart from the others. His spear was standing up in the ground beside him and a jug of water was lying by his head.

Very cautiously, without making a sound, David pulled the spear out of the ground and lifted the jug of water to his own shoulder. Then he turned and stepped softly back between the sleeping bodies over which he had so carefully come until he saw Abishai. The two then found their way together out of the camp and back up the mountainside to their own place of hiding.

By that time it was beginning to be daylight. When morning was fully come, David boldly stood out on the top of the cliff where he could be seen from below, and called in a loud voice:

"Hear! Hear! Captain of the King's army!"

Soon an answering call came from the opposite hill: "Who is calling?"

"I am David, the outlaw you are hunting! Tell me, why did you not keep better guard over your King? Two men crept into your camp last night and might have killed your master. You did not even wake up. See, in my right hand is the King's spear and in my left hand is his jug of water." David's voice was clearly heard across the valley. King Saul recognized it.

"Is this you, my son David, that is calling?" asked King Saul in surprise.

"It is my voice, my lord, O King," answered David. "Why are you following me? What have I done to you?

What wrong have I been guilty of? Let my lord, the King, listen to me! You have been hunting me as you would hunt a wild bird in the forest to shoot it. Why do you do this? Why not let me come back and live and die among my own people? I have been kind to you this night. I have saved your life when I might easily have killed you. You should be kind to me in return."

On hearing these words from David himself, King Saul felt full of shame. He hung his head and for a while he walked back and forth nervously. Then he turned, and for a moment stood still. He lifted his head, looked up toward the top of the cliff and called again:

"I have done wrong, my son David. Come back home, for I will no longer do you any harm. You spared my life last night. I will spare yours. From now on you shall be safe."

David was satisfied. He called back:

"Here is the King's spear. Let one of your men come up the mountain and get it." King Saul called back:

"Keep the spear and the jug, my son, in memory of last night. Some day you shall do great things."

After this King Saul and his men broke up their camp and went back home. David and his men, however, remained in hiding for a while longer.

What King Saul and Jonathan had both expected did come true. After some years David became King of his people.

Damon
and
Pythias

A Story from Greece

MANY YEARS AGO there lived in Greece two young men whose names were Damon and Pythias. They were good friends, and loved and trusted each other like brothers.

At that time the city of Syracuse in Sicily was ruled by a tyrant, King Dionysius. Today we would call him a dictator for he had forced the people to make him King and he ruled with a cruel hand. Dictators fear and punish people who tell them unpleasant truths. Therefore, when Pythias dared to oppose Dionysius he was condemned to death.

Brave Pythias was willing to die for the sake of what he believed to be right, but he was eager first to say good-by to his parents who lived in another part of the country. He looked King Dionysius in the eye and said:

"Your Highness, you have the power to take my life. But I beg you to grant me one request. Before I die, give me one week to go home to say good-by to my parents, and to arrange for their comfort and safety. I promise I will return by the end of the week."

"Pythias, do you take me for a fool? If I let you go, you will never come back." Proudly Pythias tossed back his head:

"You have my promise. I do not break a promise."

"Fine words! Fine words! But life is sweet. Once out of Syracuse, you will never return!" At this Damon interrupted. He had listened quietly but now could no longer keep silent:

"King Dionysius, Pythias has never broken his word. He *will* come back. To prove my faith, I will go to prison in his place, and die for him if he does not return." An ugly smile lit the face of the tyrant.

"So be it! You may take his place. But expect no mercy. If he is not back by sundown on the seventh day from now, *you die.*" Damon cast a loving look at Pythias and said:

"I'm not afraid. He will return."

Damon was led away to prison and Pythias hastened to his parents to plan for their well-being and to say a sad good-by.

The trip home went smoothly. The skies were sunny and the streams easy to ford. Pythias was a good runner. In two days he reached home.

With breaking hearts his parents heard the reason for his visit. They did not try to hold him. He had learned his high sense of honor from them. After a few hours of planning and weeping, his mother said:

"Now you must go. Damon lingers in prison until you

get back." The parents both gave him their blessing and he was speedily on his way.

Suddenly the weather changed. Storm clouds gathered. An inky darkness covered the sky. Soon lightning zigzagged and thunder clapped and roared. Then a torrent of rain descended and drenched Pythias to the skin. His garments clung about his legs. It was difficult to run. The streams turned into rivers and these rivers soon overflowed their banks and washed away the bridges. Where Pythias had walked through fords, he now had to swim against a rushing current. Precious time slipped by and Syracuse was still far away. A horrible fear gripped him. Would he get back in time?

The morning of the last day came. King Dionysius went early to the prison and entered the cell where Damon lay upon a bed of straw. A smile of evil triumph distorted his lips:

"The last day has come, Damon." His prisoner replied cheerfully:

"It is still but morning. Sundown is the appointed time."

"You do not mean that you still expect Pythias?"

"Indeed I do! He will be here by sundown!"

"Amuse yourself with your fairy tale a few hours more. It may help you to forget that when the sun sinks behind the clouds today . . . you die!"

The hours passed. A crowd began to gather to watch the execution. "Too bad," they said, "an innocent man is to die. Of course he was a fool to expect that his friend would return—yet he was a noble fool. Too bad! Too bad! Will his courage hold out to the end?"

Now the guards were leading Damon from the prison. They paused before the special seat prepared so that King Dionysius could watch the execution in comfort.

"Pythias has not returned, Damon." In a clear voice that rang through the court Damon answered:

"He will still come or else you will soon learn that he has died on the way. Tell him that I went to my death in the sure knowledge that he had not betrayed me." The light of faith that glorified Damon's face caused Dionysius to lower his eyes. Suddenly a guard shouted:

"A man comes running—he seems exhausted! He stumbles! He falls! He rises again!" All waited in hushed silence. Then, with a last great burst of effort, Pythias entered the gate, and dropped before the throne of Dionysius. As he panted the words, "Your Highness, I am back!" a mighty shout of joy arose from the throng.

With amazement and awe King Dionysius gazed on the fallen man. A new belief crept into his heart. He had seen a love and a loyalty that were stronger than the fear of death.

He rose from his chair. Above the shouts of the tumult his voice rang out: "Pythias, you have come back to live, not to die. Two such true friends must not be parted."

The Camel Driver
in Need of a Friend

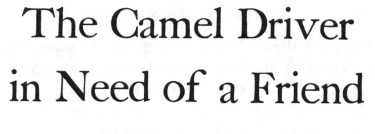

A Story from the Arabs

A MAN WAS SITTING on top of a stone fence that separated his orchard from the road. A camel driver with his herd of camels came walking by. One of the camels reached his long neck over the stone fence and pulled down the branch of one of the fruit trees and broke it off with his teeth.

The angry owner snatched up a stone and threw it at the camel and unexpectedly killed it. When the camel driver saw the camel lying dead in the road, he too picked up a stone and threw it in anger at the man on the fence. Unfortunately he hit the man in the forehead and killed him instantly.

Frightened by his rash act the camel driver jumped on the swiftest of his camels and got away as fast as he could, leaving the rest of the herd to shift for themselves.

Word of this double tragedy spread quickly through the village. The camel driver was chased, caught and taken before the Caliph. The sons of the dead man were there and demanded that the camel driver be punished with death, and that his execution take place at once.

When the camel driver saw that there was nothing he could do to save himself, and that death was certain for him, he began to think of things he wished he had done at home before coming to the town with his camels. He decided he must make one last request of the Caliph.

"Your Highness, I beg you to give me three days' time before you end my life. I need to go back home to my family and arrange several important matters. I promise you that I will return before the three days have passed. Then I shall be ready to pay the penalty I deserve for my rash deed." The Caliph suspected the man of trying to run away.

"You must have someone who will stand surety for you while you are gone. Someone here must promise to die in your place if you do not come back in three days. Otherwise I cannot trust your word."

The poor camel driver looked despairingly around on the crowd that had gathered. They were all complete strangers to him. How could he hope that any one of them would risk his life for a person he had never seen before?

The officer was already tying the man's hands behind his back. Soon he would be kneeling on the rug, waiting for the executioner's ax. In desperation he called:

"Are the people all dead who can be noble?" No answer. Again he cried even louder: "Are the people all dead who can be noble?" The crowd moved nervously and grumbled:

"He's looking for a fool!" "The man he killed was given no second chance." "I wouldn't risk an hour's wages for him." Others cried: "Off with his head!"

In the midst of the hubbub, to the great surprise of everybody, a man did come forward and stand before the Caliph. One long sigh of distress rose from everyone when they recognized who it was—their favorite teacher, Abu Dhur, truly the noblest man among them.

"Abu Dhur, our teacher! Abu Dhur, the faithful follower of the great Mohammed!" The people cried in distress. "No! No! Don't do it, Abu Dhur. We need you. Don't risk your life for this scoundrel!" But Abu Dhur was not so easily turned from his purpose. He said:

"Your Highness, let me be surety for this man."

"Don't be foolish, Abu Dhur," said the Caliph. "Do you realize that if this stranger does not keep his word and does not return, you will then have to be punished in his place?"

"I know it, your Highness. But I am ready."

The camel driver was set free, and started off at a run and was soon out of sight, while Abu Dhur was led off to prison. The excited crowd scattered to their homes.

The three days passed; the evening hour came. The manslayer had not returned. Nobody had really believed that he would. The sons of the dead man were gathered before the Caliph. They were demanding that some life must be taken in payment for the life of their father.

The Caliph was distressed. Many a time the good Abu Dhur had been of great service to him. The Caliph respected him highly and loved him for his goodness. But the Caliph had warned Abu Dhur that he would have to

be executed if the slayer did not return; and the Caliph felt
he had to keep his word.

So Abu Dhur was brought out of his prison. His hands
were tied behind his back and he was led to the place of
execution. But just as the executioner was about to raise
his ax, a loud cry came from the back of the crowd:

"Stop! Stop! Someone comes running this way!"

The Caliph gave the signal to the executioner to wait.
The crowd watched anxiously. When they saw the runner
and recognized him as the camel driver a shout of relief
rose from the crowd. The runner dropped on his knees before the Caliph and gasped: "Thank God! I am on time."

"But what a fool you are!" said the Caliph in surprise.
"Why did you return? If you had stayed away you would
have been free." The camel driver rose to his feet and stood
face to face with the Caliph and said:

"Your Highness, I have come back in order to prove
that not only are there still in the world men who are noble,
but that there are still in the world those who are truthful."

"Why then did you go away at all?" asked the Caliph.

"Your Highness, I asked for three days' stay of my sentence because I was needed at home. Some time ago a poor
widow came to me and entrusted some articles of value to
my keeping. Since I had to leave home on business, I took
her things and hid them under a great rock in a spot which
no one but myself could find. Then this dreadful thing happened to me. If you had not spared my life three days ago,
I should have died with a heavy heart, knowing that my
friend, the widow, would lose all her treasure. She would
have cursed my children because of their father, and they
could have done nothing to right the wrong. Now, how-

ever, I have given the precious things back to the widow
and I have arranged my own family affairs as best I could.
Now I can die in peace." On hearing the man's strange
story, the Caliph turned to Abu Dhur and said:

"Is this man a friend of yours?"

"No," replied Abu Dhur. "I never set eyes on him until
three days ago."

"Why then have you been such a fool as to risk your
life for the sake of a stranger? You know you would have
died had he not returned."

"Your Highness," said Abu Dhur, "I did so in order
that the camel driver would know that there are still those
who can be noble and who ask no reward for their noble-
ness."

The Caliph sat for some moments without saying a
word. The executioner unbound Abu Dhur and walked
over to the camel driver and began binding his hands behind his back.

The Caliph turned to the camel driver, who was already
kneeling on the mat with the executioner standing beside
him ready to do his work.

"I pardon you!" said the Caliph.

"Why so?" an old man from the crowd called out in
protest. And the Caliph answered:

"I pardon this man because I see now that there are still
in the world those who are noble. There are those also who
are truthful. There are those also who can be trusted to
carry the responsibility given to them. It remains for me
to show that there are still those who can be forgiving. I,
therefore, pardon this man who in anger killed another. I
myself shall pay the fine to the dead man's relatives."

Wise King Solomon

A Story from Palestine

KING DAVID WAS AN OLD MAN and knew that it would not be long before he would die. So he called his favorite son, Solomon, to him and said:

"Solomon, my son, the day of my dying is near. You must take my place when I am gone, and be King of our people. Be strong, then, my son, and show yourself a man. Do what is right. Follow the laws of God as they have been written down for us so that our people may live together in peace and their work may prosper."

Not long after this King David died, and his young son, Solomon, was made King in his place. Since the young man was very eager to be a good King, the first thing he did, after being crowned, was to go to the temple and pray God to help him.

Soon after that, King Solomon had a dream in the night. In his dream he thought he saw God and he thought he heard God speak to him, saying: "Solomon, what do you wish for more than anything else in the world?" Solomon answered God and said:

"O God, I have now been made King of this great people, but I feel I know so little. What I wish for most of all, O God, is a wise and understanding mind, so that I can do what is best for my people. I want to be able to know clearly what is right and what is wrong so that I may be fair to all." God was pleased with Solomon's wish and answered him, saying:

"You have wished well, my son. You might have wished for riches, or you might have wished for a long life, or you might have wished that all your enemies might be killed. Since you have not wished for any of these things, but have wished for a wise and understanding mind, you shall become wiser than any king who has ever lived before you.

"You shall also have what you have not wished for. You shall become very rich and if you will do what is right, you shall live a long life in peace and honor." Solomon then awoke, and realized that it had all been a dream.

But there was a great deal in King Solomon's dream that actually came true. He became very famous for his wisdom. He became very rich and he ruled a prosperous and peaceful country for many years.

Many stories have been told about him to show how wisely he settled the quarrels that were brought to him. This is, perhaps, the most famous of all the stories.

Two women came to King Solomon's court and stood before his throne. One carried a baby in her arms, the other came empty-handed. The woman without a baby was the first to tell her story.

"O King, this other woman here and I have been living together in the same house. For many months all went well with us. We were very good friends, but now we are in trouble. Not long ago I had a baby. Three days after my baby was born, this other woman also had a baby. We were both very happy.

"But one night, O King, this other woman's baby died while we were both asleep. In the middle of the night its mother awoke and discovered that her baby was dead. She was so upset, I think she did not know what she was doing. She must have felt she could not bear for me to have a living baby while hers was dead. I know it was hard. But, your Majesty, she should not have done the terrible thing she did. She rose very quietly so as not to waken me, and came over to my bed. She picked up my sleeping baby and took it away and put it in her own bed. Then she picked up the body of her dead child and brought it over and laid it down beside me while I was still asleep. She thought I would not know her baby from mine. Then she lay down again in her bed and quietly waited.

"Early in the morning, O King, while the room was still half dark, I woke up to feed my baby from my breasts, and I found he would not eat. His body was limp. I shook him and tried to waken him, but I could not, for he was dead. Then I looked more carefully into the child's face. I saw at once that it was not my baby at all, but hers that I had.

"I rose and went angrily to her bed to look at the baby she was feeding. I knew at once, O King, that the living child in her arms was mine and not hers. I knew it by its face, O King, and by its eyes, and by the way it held its little hand at her breast.

"Then I spoke crossly, O King. I accused her of having stolen my child, but she denied having done anything. She said: 'The dead son is yours and this living baby is mine.' And I said: 'No! The living baby is mine and the dead one is yours.' But she would not give me back my child. So, O King, we have been quarreling day and night ever since. But your Majesty is wise. You can see what the truth is. I beg you to judge rightly between us."

Scarcely had the first woman finished her story when the other one began. She insisted that the living baby in her arms was her own child. She denied that her baby had died in the night. And so the quarreling began again right before the King. Presently King Solomon called an officer and said:

"Fetch me a sword." When the officer entered with the sword, the King said:

"Take the baby away from this woman and cut it with

this sword into two equal parts and give one half of the child to each woman."

Scarcely had King Solomon spoken when the woman who had first told her story fell on her knees and wept. "O my Lord," she cried, "Give the child to her! Give the child to her!"

But the other woman with the baby in her arms reached out to give her baby to the officer. "Your Majesty," she said, "you are a wise King. Let it be as you have spoken."

Immediately King Solomon realized that he had discovered the true mother. He commanded the officer to take the sword away.

"Give the baby to the woman who has begged for his life. She is the real mother for she has shown true love for the child."

The story of these two women and their babies and of King Solomon's wise decision was told and retold in every village of the land. It was all a man needed to tell to prove the great wisdom of their King.

This story is still being told. Both young and old want to hear it again and again for a different reason. This story reminds us that truly good mothers love not only their own children but love the children in other families as well.

Jesus at a Wedding Party

A Story from Palestine

JESUS WAS A CARPENTER by trade. His father before him had been a carpenter all his life. Everybody expected that Jesus also would always be a carpenter. But to their surprise Jesus decided to give up his carpentering, and even to leave home in order to become a traveling teacher.

How he earned his living we do not know. Beside teaching he may have done some kind of work with his hands. Since he never stayed long in any one place he probably had to be ready to do almost anything.

In his traveling around, however, Jesus made a great many friends. There were people in almost every town who were willing to give him a bite to eat and a place to sleep. As Jesus became more widely known people even clamored for a chance to have him in their homes.

Jesus was not like our teachers today. He had no schoolhouse. His pupils were grown-up people. His teaching was done anywhere people wanted to sit down together and talk. Sometimes this would be at a dinner table. Sometimes it would be outdoors on a hillside, or it might be in a market place in the evening when the hurly-burly of marketing was over.

People liked Jesus because he was interested in the things they did and the things that they knew about, such as fishing and farming and building and even baking bread. They could tell he was interested by the way he talked.

They also liked the kind of stories he told. Nor were they afraid of him. He made them feel easy with him. He encouraged them to ask questions. And the answers Jesus gave — well, they marveled at his cleverness. But it was more than smartness. Jesus seemed to think of things no one else thought about, and he seemed to care for poor people whom others forgot or snubbed.

This is one of the stories about Jesus that has been much enjoyed.

A certain rich man's daughter was about to be married. Her father had invited many guests to come to the wedding. Since Jesus was in the town he was also invited to come, and he was happy to join in the occasion. A long table in the rich man's dining hall was piled with delicious foods.

Now, in those days at such parties the host usually planned ahead just where the most important guests were to sit at the table. At a wedding party it was thought that those seated nearest to the bride and groom were the most honored guests. The host himself would sit at the opposite end of the table in the least honored place.

Jesus and his group of special friends watched the guests as they came into the dining hall to take their seats. Some

rushed ahead of the host and took seats as near the places
for the bride and groom as they dared. Others waited to be
told where to sit.

Later when the host came in and wanted to arrange the
people at the table as he had planned, he had to go to this
one and to that one and say:

"I'm sorry, my friend, but I shall have to ask you to sit
farther along down the table."

Jesus was watching the faces of those who had to move.
There were tight lips or heads held high in the air which
seemed to say: "I'm just as good as he." Some hung their
heads as if ashamed of themselves. Jesus was quite sure
there were others who were feeling jealous, even though
they said nothing and tried to hide their feelings.

After the party was all over Jesus and a few of his
friends got together in Peter's courtyard and talked everything over. Jesus said some startling things that evening,
which his friends could not forget. First of all he made
some suggestions for the next time they were invited to a
party. He said:

"When you are invited to a feast, don't try to edge your
way into the best seat at the table, for some person more important than you in the eyes of your host may come in. If
you have seated yourself near the most honored guest it
will be embarrassing if your host comes to you and says:
'I'm sorry, but I must give this man your place.' You will
feel ashamed of yourself when you move down to a lower
seat.

"I suggest that, when you are invited to a feast, you go
and stand by the seat intended for the least important person. Your host may come to you later and say: 'My friend,

please move up closer to the honored guest!' Then you will feel happy to be so honored.

"It is well to remember that everyone that exalts himself shall be humbled. The one who keeps himself humble, shall be exalted."

Then Jesus had another thought for those who gave parties. He said this to them:

"When you make a dinner or a supper, don't always invite just your own friends or relatives or your rich neighbors. You know that if you invite them they will some day give a dinner for you in return. Are you not then merely exchanging gifts?

"I suggest that, when you give a party, you invite some poor people who can't ask you to come to dinner at their homes. Ask a lame person or a blind person who can't prepare a meal for you. They won't pay you back with a dinner, but you will feel happy in seeing their enjoyment, and you will find that in the long run you will be rewarded.

"If you love only those who love you, what thanks should you be given for that?

"If you do good only to those who do good to you, what thanks should you be given for that? Even bad people do that.

"Let us, in our kindness, be like God—the Father of us all. Remember, He makes the sun shine on good and bad alike. He sends rain both on the just and on the unjust.

"Let us then include in our kindnesses everybody, as God does."

Teacher's Guide

by Patricia Hoertdoerfer

How to Use These Stories

You can create different types of educational programs around the forty-two stories in this collection. A year-long program can be enriched by some of the creative movements, games and social action projects suggested in the teacher's guide. A half-year program could highlight human relationships or abiding questions. A four- to six-week program might focus on one unit, such as the wonders of birth or human ideals or the mysteries of death. If time is limited, you could use a single story program/worship service that focuses on a specific issue, question or theme.

A sample program could open with a session focused on the proverb, "Under one sky all people are one family." A large globe or map could be used to point out the various countries/lands where these stories originated. A display table of resources, books, pictures, artifacts, art and music from the different countries could be explored. A closing session or celebration could again focus on the proverb with the children's experiences highlighted and creative expressions around many stories displayed.

A final session could celebrate all the stories in this book and the Unitarian Universalist values the children have learned. It could be inspired by the children and facilitated by the teacher, and should represent the fruition of the year's experiences. Hopefully, the children will feel that they have received a precious heritage that will enrich their lives.

Another way of sequencing these stories for use in a program is to select a country and for several sessions tell stories from that country. A display table could accumulate many items brought from home that depict family travels and/or ancestry, as well as children's creations reflecting the themes of the stories.

You should adapt, change or keep the stories as needed. For example, you could modify the story, "The Blind Men and The Elephant," by saying the men went to a wise *woman* and respected teacher instead of a man for answers to their questions. Another example would be the story "A Visit To The Land-of-Great-Men," which could be changed to "A Visit To The Land-of-Great-People." You could highlight the beauty of a rainbow-colored cloud instead of an unclear and ambiguous cloud in the original story.

If at all possible, familiarize yourself with the entire collection of stories before launching any program based on these tales. General knowledge of plot, important issues and personalities, background culture and religion are a great resource for you to draw on during discussions, activities and worship time. The table of contents and the teacher's guide contain helpful outlines and summaries of story themes and origins.

It is important for you to understand and know the interests and needs of your specific group of participants. Generally speaking, seven to nine year olds love stories and recognize themselves as well as others' rights and worth in and through stories. But story discussion time needs to be brief and alternated with activities that allow for movement, games, drama, crafts, songs.

Children this age are full of wonder. They are ready to open up to the larger world and to ask fresh new questions. Again and again they will ask, "Are these stories true?" or "Is this story real?" Your response could start the discussion: "Let's find out. Let's see which parts are true and which parts are make-believe." Or "What do you think?" You need to help children figure out their own answers by engaging their new mental abilities (analytical and verbal thinking) along with their imaginative abilities. Children learn at an early age that all humans are imperfect and that we can all learn from past mistakes as well as achievements. Given stimulation and a sympathetic environment, children can begin to work out their own creative answers to life's big questions.

At this age children are searching for their own identity and they are often delighted to hear about children from different cultures and countries struggling with similar life experiences and situations. They will be quick to discover how much alike people are everywhere in the things that matter most, from friendship and love to justice, truth and beauty.

Children enjoy rituals, opportunities for reverence and experiences of wonder that enhance the meanings of these stories. Worship services and acts of kindness and social service as a family, religious education class or intergenerational community will cultivate a tangible sense of "the human universals that bind us together in a common world."

The discussion questions in the teacher's guide offer many

possible points to enhance the spiritual and ethical meanings of Fahs's stories as they pertain to today's children. But there are more discussion questions than any teacher or parent would care to ask. Some of the questions may not be appropriate to your group of children or particular congregation, and too many questions may crowd out the children's opportunity to express their own insights.

This teacher's guide, as any curriculum, guide or manual, is a springboard, a starting place. You are invited to adapt stories, discussion questions and program activities by using your own creative imagination and the special talents of your congregation.

Some teachers may want to follow the order in which the stories already appear in this book. The units on Abiding Questions, Birth and Death, Human Universals and Human Diversity offer a natural sequence ranging from cosmic issues to earthly and human concerns.

On the other hand some teachers may want to arrange the sequence of stories to fit current world problems or children's particular needs. The following two sections outline different situations and ways of living for each story, as well as stories by characters, that you may find useful. These groupings of stories are reprinted from the original edition of *From Long Ago and Many Lands*.

The Stories Grouped to Suggest Different Situations and Ways of Living

1. THESE DISCOVERED WAYS TO A MORE FRIENDLY WORLD
    The Picture on the Kitchen Wall   *A Story from China*
    The Jewish Traveler and the Robbers   *A Story from Palestine*
    The Dog and the Heartless King   *A Story from India*
    The Very Short Rule   *A Story from Palestine*

2. THESE WERE AFRAID
    The Nervous Little Rabbit   *A Story from India*
    The Boy Who Was Afraid to Try   *A Story from Uganda*

3. THESE THOUGHT QUARRELING AND FIGHTING WERE THE ONLY WAYS
   The Blind Men and the Elephant   *A Story from India*
   The Complaint against the Stomach   *A Story from Greece*
   A Ring-around of Temper   *A Story from Burma*
   The Trees Choose a King   *A Story from Palestine*
   The Blind Man and the Lame Man   *A Story from Uganda*

4. THESE TRIED SOMETHING NEW
   The Bell of Atri   *A Story from Sicily*
   The King Who Changed His Mind   *A Story from India*
   The Naumburg Children's Festival   *A Story from Germany*

5. THESE DREAMED OF A BETTER COUNTRY
   A Visit to the Land-of-Great-Men   *A Story from China*

6. THESE WANTED TO BE BIGGER, STRONGER OR HAPPIER
   THAN OTHERS
   The Whale and the Big Bronze Statue   *A Story from Japan*
   The Richest King in the World   *A Story from Greece*
   The Wind and the Sun   *A Story from Greece*
   Jesus at a Wedding Party   *A Story from Palestine*

7. THESE COULD NOT DECIDE
   The Miller, His Boy and Their Donkey   *A Story from Greece*
   The Wee, Wise Bird   *A Story Told by Jewish Rabbis*

8. THESE NEEDED A FRIEND
   The Two Friends   *A Story from India*
   King Saul Finds a Harpist   *A Story from Palestine*
   David and Jonathan Become Friends   *A Story from Palestine*
   The King's Spear and Water Jug   *A Story from Palestine*
   Damon and Pythias   *A Story from Greece*
   The Camel Driver in Need of a Friend   *A Story from the Arabs*
   Wise King Solomon   *A Story from Palestine*

9. THESE TRIED TO CHEAT
   Who Ate the Squabs?   *A Story from Czechoslovakia*

The Two Cheats *A Story from Uganda*
The Old Bowl *A Story from India*

10. THESE ASKED QUESTIONS EVERYBODY WANTS TO ASK
The Persevering Ant *A Story from South America*
Gautama Finds Out for Himself *A Story from India*
The Mustard-Seed Medicine *A Story from India*
The Musician and His Trumpet *A Story from India*
The Road to Olelpanti *A Story from North America*
The Fig Seed *A Story from India*
The Lump of Salt *A Story from India*
The Questions of King Milinda *A Story from India*

11. THESE WERE THOUGHT TO BE TOO GOOD TO BE
MERE HUMAN BEINGS
The Birth of Jesus *A Story from Palestine*
The Birth of Buddha *A Story from India*
The Birth of Confucius *A Story from China*

The Stories Grouped By Characters

1. LEGENDS OF CERTAIN GREAT MEN
The Picture on the Kitchen Wall *A Story from China*
The Very Short Rule *A Story from Palestine*
The King Who Changed His Mind *A Story from India*
The Richest King in the World *A Story from Greece*
Jesus at a Wedding Party *A Story from Palestine*
King Saul Finds a Harpist *A Story from Palestine*
David and Jonathan Become Friends *A Story from Palestine*
The King's Spear and Water Jug *A Story from Palestine*
Wise King Solomon *A Story from Palestine*
Gautama Finds Out for Himself *A Story from India*

2. STORIES TOLD BY GREAT MEN
The Jewish Traveler and the Robbers *A Story Jesus Told*
The Dog and the Heartless King *A Story Buddha Told*
The Blind Men and the Elephant *A Story Buddha Told*
The Mustard-Seed Medicine *A Story Buddha Told*

3. LEGENDS OF OTHER PEOPLE—NOT SO FAMOUS
    The Boy Who Was Afraid to Try   *A Story from Uganda*
    The Blind Man and the Lame Man   *A Story from Uganda*
    The Bell of Atri   *A Story from Sicily*
    The Naumburg Children's Festival   *A Story from Germany*
    A Visit to the Land-of-Great-Men   *A Story from China*
    The Miller, His Boy and Their Donkey   *A Story from Greece*
    Damon and Pythias   *A Story from Greece*
    The Camel Driver in Need of a Friend   *A Story from the Arabs*
    Who Ate the Squabs?   *A Story from Czechoslovakia*
    The Two Cheats   *A Story from Uganda*
    The Old Bowl   *A Story from India*
    A Musician and His Trumpet   *A Story from India*
    The Fig Seed   *A Story from India*
    The Lump of Salt   *A Story from India*
    The Questions of King Milinda   *A Story from India*

4. ANCIENT FABLES, MOSTLY ABOUT IMAGINARY ANIMALS
    The Dog and the Heartless King   *A Story from India*
    The Nervous Little Rabbit   *A Story from India*
    The Complaint against the Stomach   *A Story from Greece*
    A Ring-around of Temper   *A Story from Burma*
    The Trees Choose a King   *A Story from Palestine*
    The Whale and the Big Bronze Statue   *A Story from Japan*
    The Wind and the Sun   *A Story from Greece*
    The Wee, Wise Bird   *A Story Told By Jewish Rabbis*
    The Two Friends   *A Story from India*
    The Persevering Ant   *A Story from South America*
    The Road to Olelpanti   *A Story from North America*

5. WONDER TALES OF THE BIRTHDAYS OF THREE VERY GREAT MEN
    The Birth of Jesus   *A Story from Palestine*
    The Birth of Buddha   *A Story from India*
    The Birth of Confucius   *A Story from China*

The Art of Storytelling

Become Acquainted With the Story

First, you need to read the story you are going to tell in order to appreciate and enjoy it. You should then read it again twice, each time visualizing the incidents more and more vividly as dramatic pictures and happenings. Make note of the story's plot development, from the introduction of the situation through the conflict, suspense, climax and solution. Visualize these developments as graphic pictures that you can portray in words, as a work of art just as truly as the painting of a picture by line and color.

Remember the Story Details

Many of the best storytellers leave room for something new in each telling. Be a watchful teacher and see whether you have made your point, whether the group is "with you." You should feel free to alter the story's words, to emphasize a thought, to ease up or increase an emotional effect according to the response you meet in the faces and the attention of the group. It is a mistake to memorize a story in such a way that the wording is not flexible or cannot be manipulated to meet your needs.

As a skilled storyteller, Sophia Lyon Fahs carefully prepared the stories in this volume for a given age. You will probably want to make a few changes as you retell these stories. After repeated readings, you will find that the words have become your own without any special effort at memorizing.

Practice Storytelling

When you are familiar with a story, you need to consider ways to make the best oral presentation. Your voice can be an effective tool when storytelling. You need to practice modulating your voice as well as raising and lowering its volume. After awhile you develop a sense of when to give accent to certain words, when to speak rapidly, when to repeat and when to pause. Other tools of expression can be incorporated, such as a gesture, a wondering look or a smile. A hat, scarf or other item of clothing can enhance the drama of the story.

Through thoughtful and continued practice, you can hone your skills of storytelling. You need to constantly evaluate each practice rendition from your audience's point of view. Will they understand and enjoy the story?

When it's time to tell your story to your class (or family), let the story develop with your audience. Respond to the children's reactions and adjust the timing, details or even the props as you go along. Perhaps more can be made vivid to the senses; children especially respond to what they can see, hear, smell, feel and taste.

Each attempt at storytelling should be regarded as an opportunity for learning. After your story hour, you can take time to think over what happened, what you did and how the children acted. Our mistakes sometimes teach us more than our successes.

Participatory Storytelling

Instead of telling the story yourself, you can engage the children in reading the lines of different characters or in recounting various episodes of the story. Allowance must be made for the children's range of reading skills. Participation by invitation, matching reading skills to character or story sections and adequate preparation time will enhance the success of a cooperative endeavor in storytelling.

But whether you tell the story or the children participate in the storytelling, each story needs to engage children in thought-provoking ways. Their response and participation with zest and intelligence will ensure a lively and meaningful discussion.

Leading Discussions

Some of the stories in this collection are very simple and their meaning can be summed up in a few words or in some wise statement. You should refrain from stating the moral of each story. Let the children discover it themselves. Sometimes you can pose a puzzling problem or question to help the children think through an answer. In some cases, when the children have caught the story's meaning, you can write on newsprint a proverb or wise saying that sums it up and post it where it can be seen and reread from time to time.

After each story, pause and invite children to tell you what they heard. Often their immediate response is, "Is it true?" You could answer, "Let's find out. Let's see if we can name which parts are true and which parts are make-believe. What do you think?"

The first questions you ask should focus on the problems and difficulties that the characters in the stories had to face. Later questions should deal with the solutions that were tried and should encourage opinions about these solutions. For example:

- Docs the story remind you of another story we have had before? In what ways is this one different?
- Does the story remind you of anything that ever happened to you or any trouble or difficulty you ever had to meet? What was your experience?
- Is there anything about this story that puzzled you?
- Do you care to ask a question about it?
- You seemed to be listening while I told the story. Which part of it was the most exciting? Why was this?
- What else might have happened? What would you have thought of the character if that had happened?
- Why do you think this story has been told over and over for hundreds of years to children?

Seven-, eight- and nine-year-old children are capable of engaging in meaningful and productive discussions. The length of their discussions will vary depending on their maturity and the effectiveness of the adult leadership.

Many of the stories in this collection, except the simple parables, have more than one significant moral. A thoughtful teacher will find something more each time she or he reviews one of them. But when discussing the stories with children, use only those insights that are within the children's range of comprehension and appreciation. Remember the following:

- Keep the discussion on the children's level. Insist that they speak from their own experiences and from their previous learnings.
- Let the discussion be pertinent to the children's home, school, neighborhood and Unitarian Universalist community experiences.
- Beware of the loquacious child who wishes to talk all the time. Even if she or he is your "best pupil," monitor her or him and see that others have a chance to speak. Draw out the shy, silent child by directing questions to her or him. Do not be discouraged by a child's mumbled, "I don't know." Do not press or embarrass her or him, but after a time turn to the child again and say, "Remember, Jean/Jimmy when we . . . " Entice children to express themselves.

To Enrich Your Program

Environment
The room environment can enhance the concepts, values and enjoyment of these stories. Displaying art objects, artifacts and souvenirs from the various cultures in these stories will add tremendously to children's experiences. A good introduction for children would be telling several stories in succession from the same country in order to let the display table grow.

Pictures of India, China, Palestine and Africa will enrich imaginations and add color to the stories. Simple books about these different peoples may be enjoyed as outside reading. Pottery, fabrics, curious nuts and other objects may be collected. Enjoying the various forms of beauty that come from different lands will increase the children's respect for the people who have created this beauty.

Maps and atlases need to be in the classroom to reference each story's culture or country of origin. If desired a bulletin board entitled "Where in the world?" could be used. On it pictures, newspaper or magazine clippings and even original poetry about these countries and people, contributed by the children and their families, would enrich the experience for all.

Dramatics

Most modern educators agree that we learn most effectively by doing. Many of these stories lend themselves to creative drama.

There is a great range of possibilities for drama activities. Simple role playing of leading characters in consecutive incidents can spontaneously come together in a single session. Children just need a corner or rug or chair and their imaginations do the rest.

A full-scale dramatic play and performance is also a grand educational project. Planning the scenes, selecting the actors, making the costumes, constructing the properties and painting the scenery can be a valuable way for children to use their imaginations. But projects should remain simple and within the children's abilities, and should not be too time-consuming.

In planning a play it is necessary to give children a little idea of dramatic form. Help them to choose a few scenes. Show them how they can introduce other needed information through conversation and other means that may suggest themselves. Suppose, for example, that in "King Saul Finds a Harpist" you decide that the first scene should be David's initial visit to King Saul. You could begin with King Saul alone on the stage. He sits in a dejected mood. Two servants glance at him from the side and say:

"Poor, poor King Saul. He used to be so happy. Now he is always sad. I remember how bravely he led the army against the Philistines. He held his head so high. Look at him now."

"Let us hope that the new medicine will help him."

"Medicine? I didn't know there was any."

"Not real medicine. I meant the harpist who is coming to play for the King. Sometimes beautiful music can make a sick mind well. His family have sent for a harpist."

"Who is he? A nobleman?"

"No, a shepherd who learned his art among the hills."

The children will quickly grasp the technique and be ready to revise their method of presentation. They will then be in a position to decide on the scenes they want, and what must be done in each. They often rely on a narrator to fill in the gaps in the story. This role, incidentally, is considered a lead and will be eagerly assumed.

Having decided on the scenes, the class can begin imagining

the setting of each one. Where does it take place? Who are the characters in it? What has just happened? How are they feeling? When the situation is clearly in the children's minds, they can resume their acting under the restrictions of a two- to three-act play.

As the play begins to take form, the group will start to be concerned about the audience. At this stage help the children to appreciate that every honest contribution is important. The servant who makes an announcement can spoil the play if he or she forgets his or her lines, or giggles, or is flippant at the wrong place. Here is a chance to learn and to practice true cooperation. Only a few children can take big parts, yet the smallest part is necessary to the whole.

There are also important parts in a play that are done behind the scenes. Children who take on these roles are not given the thrill of applause. They are the artists who paint the backdrops, make properties or do the stagecraft. They are the costume-makers who create headdresses from a band of cloth. They will take real delight in these activities and learn to work for the joy of achievement.

You will need to develop your own techniques, too. The religious value of planning, designing and performing a dramatic play are at least threefold: (1) imaginative participation in the story, (2) the joy of contributing one's best to the greatest good of a larger whole, and (3) creating something that has never been done this way before. These gains are of significant value in empowering individuals and enriching groups.

Art

When a child is allowed to express him- or herself through tempera or poster paints with a large brush on an expanse of paper, there is usually a satisfying emotional release that comes to him or her and a surge of desire to create something distinctively his or her own. This result comes, however, only when each child is given the freedom to paint as he or she thinks and feels.

Interesting and revealing experiments can be tried by asking children to paint how they once felt when they were younger and perhaps were very angry or very much afraid. It may be easier for a child to paint something from his or her past experience than to express a present emotion.

For the stories in this book, children could draw or paint different scenes of a story, a picture of something similar that happened to them, themselves in a story doing something with one of the main characters or how they can use what they learned from the story.

Children's paintings should be appreciated by adults and not judged on the basis of external reality from the adult point of view, or from adult standards of artistic merit or beauty. If children have sincerely expressed their own emotions or thoughts, their painting deserves an understanding and sympathetic acceptance.

Many different media can be used for creative expression— clay, fabrics, wood, crayons, sand, paper, charcoal, chalk. Individual expressions from clay, paper or fabric allow the natural creativity and imagination of children to grow. Group projects of murals, banners and quilts call for cooperation and responsibility.

Group artwork provides opportunities for conflict and jealousies to develop and sometimes for unexpected cooperation to appear. In tense and difficult situations, real character and religious education can occur. When these times come, ask the children to stop their painting or drawing and talk through their difficulties. Let them see the need for working their problem out together. Go through the steps of conflict resolution—name or clarify the problem, express feelings, brainstorm solutions, choose a "win/win" solution, make a common agreement on resolution and affirmation of one another. In the end these valuable experiences in cooperation may be the most important lessons learned.

Music

Music and songs can greatly enhance the experience of these stories. Some songs to sing include: "Make New Friends," "We've Got the Whole World in our Hands," "Love Is a Circle," "Under One Sky," "We Are a Gentle, Loving People" and "Go Now In Peace."

Children's Songs for a Friendly Planet, compiled by Evelyn Weiss, is a good source book for these and many more songs.

Creative Movement

Children ages seven to nine often relate to religious themes and stories on an intuitive level. Their intuitive thoughts and feelings can manifest themselves through pantomime, movement and/or dance. Children need opportunities to express themselves and communicate their understandings without words or a structured "logical" format.

For children, movement is exploration. It is a personal journey toward capabilities and strengths and limitations. Using movement activities in education ought to give the children the message that multiplicity and variety are valued.

Charades, mime, dance and other body movement experiences are good to offer throughout the program. Stories of the wonder of birth and the mysteries of death lend themselves to experiments in creative movement. Rhythm and music can enhance expressions of movement and dance. Stories on concepts of "god" and natural forces (sun and wind) are good possibilities for creative movement activities.

Games

Games can be used in a variety of ways to enrich this program. Circle games, "new games" and cooperative games could introduce, integrate or explore the themes to many of these stories. They could be used as time-out games, bridging games or improvisational games to complement any session.

Some resources are:

Fluegelman, Andrew, ed. *More New Games and Playful Ideas.* New York, NY: Doubleday, 1981.

Fluegelman, Andrew, ed. *The New Games Book.* Tiburon, CA: The Headlands Press, Inc., 1975.

Grunfeld, Frederic. *Games of the World.* New York, NY: Plenary Publications International, Inc., 1975.

Rice, Wayne and Mike Yaconelli. *Play It!* Grand Rapids, MI: Zondervan Publishing, 1986.

Rice, Wayne and Mike Yaconelli. *Play It Again!* Grand Rapids, MI: Zondervan Publishing, 1993.

Social Service/Social Action Projects
There are many opportunities to include a social service/social action project in association with a special story theme or a particular country. UNICEF and the Unitarian Universalist Service Committee are projects suggested with "The Dog and the Heartless King" story, but could be incorporated with many other stories. Local service projects may be available through various social agencies and/or institutions. For example, Habitat for Humanity, Project on Endangered Species or centers for refugees offer many avenues for participation and service projects. Care needs to be given to ensure that the project is appropriate and that it is the children's own project and not merely that of their parents. Face-to-face encounters and hands-on experiences are especially thought-provoking and valuable.

Connections Between Home and Religious Education
There are many ways that parents and family can reinforce the meaningful experiences of these stories. In the congregation's newsletter or through letters home, the topics and stories can be named and highlighted for further discussion throughout the week. Books and resources from home can be brought into class to enhance the themes of the stories and the different cultures and peoples. Participation in class visits, field trips and class and religious education celebrations are good ways to share the richness of these stories as a family.

The parent-teacher partnership is important. You can be more effective when you know each child's needs, interests and/or problems. Parents need to know their child's teacher(s) and be as helpful as possible. Some definite ways of mutual communication include:

- Parent-teacher/family-class meetings
- Sharing resources, travel experiences
- Sharing specialized skills
- Volunteering to help with special events and/or projects.

Discussion Questions

The Abiding Questions

1. The Picture on the Kitchen Wall

This is the story of a man who lived in China in the seventh century BCE, during the reign of Emperor Kao Tsung of the Tang Dynasty. It is said that seven generations lived together harmoniously in Chang Kung's home. Just how his name became connected with the Kitchen God is not known. It is reasonable, however, to suppose that the god was once a human being of most excellent character. Pasting a new picture of the Kitchen God above the kitchen stove every new year is still a very common practice in China.

Questions

- (Contrast the American home with this Chinese home.) How many people live in your home? Who are they? (Get general responses: father, mother, brothers, sisters, sometimes one or more grandparents, an uncle or aunt.) How many lived in Chang Kung's home? How would you like to live in such a home? Would you like so many people around? What might trouble you?
- (Discuss the Chinese idea of "kindness.") What does it mean to be kind? Why is it a "golden secret?" Is Chang Kung a religious hero (trying to live what he believed and valued)? Is it possible to be kind all the time?
- (Discuss the idea of living Lives of Kindness.) Is it easy to be kind? What are some ways we can be kind to our parents, siblings, friends, teachers, pets? What acts of kindness have been done for you in the past week? How can we be kind to people we don't know? Wild animals? Precious parts of our planet earth?

2. The Jewish Traveler and The Robbers—
'The Good Samaritan'

The original rendering of this story can be found in the New Testament of the Bible: Luke 10:25-37. This is a well-known story from Jesus. The key words are "stranger and foreigner," "help and hurt" and "courage and fear."

The words "prejudice" and "stereotype" need to be defined and simply but thoroughly explained. You may want to use the following definitions:

- A prejudice is an unfavorable attitude toward or feeling about a person or group of people based on lack of knowledge and/or lack of information.
- A stereotype is a general statement about a group of people based on ignorance and/or misinformation.

Use examples applicable to the children's environment. If they are likely to have heard derogatory remarks about African Americans, Jews, Catholics, Mexicans or Japanese, use those groups closest to home for illustration. Perhaps a child has had a disagreeable experience with one individual which was transferred to a whole group. You could give other examples of stereotype/prejudice, such as "All old people are hard of hearing," "I don't like people who are tall" and "I think people who wear glasses are dumb."

Questions

- Why did these three people—rich man, temple musician, Samaritan—all hesitate before helping the Jewish merchant? (Discuss them one by one.)
- Are there certain kinds of people we might hesitate to help if they were in trouble?
- What decisions can you make about someone at school, church or in the neighborhood who looks, speaks, believes differently from you?
- Are these men at all like us?
- Why did the Samaritan decide to help the merchant?
- What do you think Jesus was trying to say through this story?

3. The Dog and the Heartless King

This is one of Buddha's parables. Consequently it is very old. But this story is timeless as well as timely because it applies to conditions in the world today.

First, the children need to understand the meaning of a parable. In a parable the storyteller puts people or animals into her or his story that are intended to remind us of something that is not a person or an animal. Perhaps the person or animal is meant to remind us of something that can't be seen at all.

The children may not have sufficient insight to name that "something." On the other hand some of them may be able to do so. The dog in this story may be intended to remind us of our *conscience*. It bothers us sometimes just as this barking dog bothered the King, and we can't be happy until our *conscience* is satisfied. Most children will understand this concept. How far you go in explaining this meaning must be left to your own best judgment, based on your understanding of the children's maturity. It will do little good to go beyond their ability to think.

This story could be followed by a service project for the hungry in your local community or participation in an interfaith food bank program. Opportunities through UNICEF (Halloween Appeal) and the Unitarian Universalist Service Committee (UUSC) "Guest at Your Table" program could be meaningful projects for your class and/or religious education program.

For further information write to: UNICEF, United Nations Building, New York, NY 10016 or UUSC, 130 Prospect Street, Cambridge, MA 02139.

Questions

- Why was the King called a "heartless King"?
- Is the barking dog a real dog?
- What needed to be done to stop this barking dog?
- Are there hungry people in the United States today? In other countries of the world today?

- What does being hungry day after day, week after week, month after month, do to children?
- Do we have any responsibility for these hungry children?

4. A Very Short Rule or 'The Golden Rule'

This story can be found in the New Testament of the Bible in the following passages: Matthew 7:12, Luke 6:31, Mark 7:1-5 and 14-23. This is a well-known story from Jesus.

If the first four stories have been read in the order used here, it would be interesting to let the children compare them. The children's preferences should be freely expressed. They will probably see a likeness in all four stories. If they also discover that one story came from China, another from India and two from Jesus and the Bible, they will begin to feel as if they belong in a great big world where people have long been trying to find some "golden secret" or rule for living that will satisfy and give meaning to life.

Questions

- All the people who talked to Jesus in this story seemed to find it hard to be good. Why was this? Do you find it hard, too? What makes it hard?
- What are some of the rules you have to obey and find hard to remember?
- What was the very short rule Jesus suggested? (Challenge the children: While one member of the class states the rule, the others try to stand on one leg.)
- How good a rule do you really think this is?
- Is it a good rule for *all* situations?
- How can you tell someone that you do not want to play or be in their group or be with them so that they will leave you alone without hurting their feelings?
- Does it deserve to be called a Golden Rule? (Help the children think through this rule in their everyday life. Ask them how it would work in specific situations.) If you wanted to give your father a birthday present, would you give him a

bicycle because you want him to give you a bike for your birthday? Or if you really want a CD player, would you give a CD player to a deaf friend? (Help the children understand that we must learn how to imagine ourselves in other people's situations in order for this rule to work well.)

5. The Boy Who Was Afraid to Try

This story comes from another land and continent, namely from Uganda in Africa. It contains some deep psychological wisdom. The kinds of fears Kumba had are connected with or caused by his relations to other people. Kumba asked two abiding questions that we ask throughout our lives: Who am I? How should I relate to and act toward others?

Questions

- Have you ever felt a little bit like Kumba?
- Let us talk about the advice the animals gave to Kumba. Do you agree with the Lion? The Antelope? The Leopard? The Elephant? The Rabbit?
- What changed Kumba from a fool to a wise and great man? Did the animals change Kumba or did he change himself?

6. The Bell of Atri

This story may well be a true story. It comes from Sicily. The story is several hundred years old but not old in the sense the Jataka tales are old or the Bible stories are old.

You can successfully introduce this story by talking briefly about different kinds of bells—church bells, school bells, fire gongs, table bells, etc.

This story lends itself to improvisational dramatics. Let one member of the class be chosen as the Judge and the rest play people living in the town. When someone thinks of an injustice that might have happened, lead him or her to a chosen spot in the room and ring an imaginary bell. Let all gather in the home of the Judge, hear the complaint and give their testimony on one side or the other.

Questions

- (After the story has been told, the children may like to talk freely about the people in the story, telling of the things they liked or did not like.) What do they think of King John's idea of a Bell of Justice?
- (Let the children imagine some of the occasions when the bell might have been rung.) Why did people often ring the bell at first and not ring it so often later?
- What if we had such a Bell of Justice in our classroom or town? When might it be rung? Has anyone been unfair recently?
- (This story also lends itself to a discussion of our treatment of animals or pets.) Suppose your cat or dog or goldfish could ring a Bell of Justice. When might they ring it?
- Can anyone be as fair as the Judge in this story? Why?

7. The King Who Changed His Mind

King Asoka, the hero of this story, was a real king who ruled a country almost as large as present-day India. He reigned during the third century BCE (from 274 to 236 BCE). His story, so far as we know, has never been retold for Western children.

The people of India recognize Asoka as one of their very great men. King Asoka was the first great Buddhist disciple to organize Buddha's followers into a missionary group. Through Asoka's zeal and leadership, Buddhism was carried northward into Kashmir and southward into Ceylon (present-day Sri-Lanka). Children should start learning about historical people like Asoka. As they mature they are likely to hear more about him and their respect for him is bound to grow.

This story of a change in ideals, from warrior to peacemaker, can be made very poignant for children.

Questions

- Was it a big change or a little bit of a change?
- Was it a hard change or an easy one?
- When Asoka changed was he doing what his mother liked or what his father would have wished him to do if he had been alive?
- Can you imagine any other people who might have criticized Asoka?
- (Children will like Asoka's independence. At this age, they are beginning to ask their own plans about what they are going to do and be. They, too, are probably going to change their plans. The future conductor will decide to run a locomotive and then in his dreams will become a flyer. Perhaps some of the children already have dreams of being a soldier. This story will challenge such an ideal.)

   Do you or do you not agree with Asoka about fighting? Do you wish there were no more soldiers or sailors to fight wars for us?

   (Encourage the children to give reasons for their opinions. Help them to realize that this question, whether to have wars or not to have wars, is the most serious question the people of the world have to face today.)
- Is the Law of Life that Buddha taught King Asoka still applicable today? Why or why not?

8. The Naumburg Children's Festival

Procop was a great general of the Hussite army in Bohemia. In the early summer of 1435 he and his army marched through the high mountain passes into Saxony, encamped on the banks of the Saale River and laid siege to the old walled German town of Naumburg. For many years the cherry festival has been celebrated annually in Naumburg. It is the proud tradition of the town.

   When the children have heard the story, ask what they like about it. The people and the scenes are easily imagined. The school teacher and the big fat general and the children will all fascinate the listeners. The story lends itself easily to dramatization.

Questions

- (Discuss war and its consequences in terms of human suffering.) How would you feel if you were a soldier going off to war to kill or perhaps be killed? How do we feel when someone we love dies?
- How do you think the general felt as he played with the children? What happens when we get to know our "enemies," or anyone we fear? Has something like that ever happened to you?
- Can anyone think of another story about a child who did something that was difficult? Or does anyone remember ever doing something their mother or father could not do?

9. The Persevering Ant

This story takes us to South America and to the Indians in the mountains of Brazil. This is a "cumulative" story, one in which a question or theme is carried throughout, building on the children's understanding.

Before telling the story, let the children know it is a parable or fable. Tell them that they will have a chance to guess who the Ant is supposed to represent. If they guess human beings, as they probably will, ask why the storyteller chose the Ant. Why not a bigger animal? This choice suggests a feeling of smallness that we all share when we are in the presence of big spaces, high mountains and the wide sky. We are all little people walking around on a big earth, and we all wonder about it and ask: What is it that is stronger than anything else? Even the Indians kept asking and asking, like the little Ant. Through this story, the children may come to sense the universality of this desire to know and understand.

Some child in the group, or the children together, might want to work out a cumulative story of their own, in which they use some other kind of animal or being to search for something stronger than itself, and goes on and on or higher and higher and in turn is led to God.

Questions

- What is the strongest thing in the world?
- Are there some questions that have no answers or that have many answers? What are some of these questions?

10. Gautama Finds Out for Himself

This is a very old story from before the time of Jesus, yet it is not a story of simple or primitive people. It is about a prince, a palace, gardens, feasting, dancing, riding with chariots and horses. Gautama renounced luxury and spent seven years seeking answers to his questions. Today he is still honored as one of the wisest men who have ever lived. This story of renunciation will stir the children.

Questions

- Gautama had the best of everything obtainable in his day. Can you name all the good things he had to make him happy? (Don't let them pass over the sports he could enjoy, the servants, the delicious food, his most beautiful wife and the little son whom he loved.)
- Why did Gautama give up all these things and go away to live under the trees, be his own servant and beg for rice to eat? (Tell the children that he wanted to find some satisfying answer to his questions about sickness, old age and death. To understand, to know, to find out what life is— all these were more important to Gautama than being with those he loved most.)

11. The Fig Seed

"The Fig Seed" and the following story, "The Lump of Salt," are from the Upanishads, which were written sometime before the sixth century BCE. "Shad" in the word "Upanishad" is from the root word that means "to sit." Therefore, these stories denote discussions between a teacher and his followers while they were sitting together.

The boy in this story, Svetakatu, was a historical character. His father's name was Vajnavalkya (Vaj-na-val'-kya). He is still remembered as one of the most distinguished philosophers of ancient Vedic India. Svetakatu also became famous as a teacher. They both lived more than a thousand years before Jesus.

This story might be introduced by giving the children some direct experience with seeds. Bring some seeds to class. Cut them open and ask the children what they can see. You could bring a microscope and let the children examine their seeds. Ask them what they see, but at this point do not press with further questions. Let them talk freely. Telling the story of Svetakatu will challenge them to think deeply.

After the story is finished be quiet for a few moments. Give an opportunity for meditation and for spontaneous remarks.

Questions

- Have you ever heard of a factory where seeds are made?
- Why not?
- What would you say is in a seed that no one can see?
- How does one know whether something is alive or dead?
- Do you agree with the father that invisible things are hidden in other things than seeds? Name some of these invisible things.

12. The Lump of Salt

Before you tell the story, conduct an experiment. Bring in a basin or wide pan and salt. Display it on a table. Ask a child to fill the pan with water and a second to drop some piece of salt into the water. Ask: Where has the salt gone?

After the experiment, read the story aloud to the class. At

the correct places in the story let different children take turns at tasting the water. Questions and remarks are likely to come quickly even before you finish telling this story. Ask the children to hear the story though before interrupting with their questions. Scientifically minded children will be quick to give their explanations in answer to the following questions. An excellent resource to have on hand is the book *Hide-and-Seek With God* by Mary Ann Moore (Boston: Skinner House Books, 1994). If there is interest and time, read or tell a few of these stories and remark that there are still mysteries beyond our understanding.

Questions

- Why does the salt dissolve? What makes it melt?
- Perhaps the father in that long-ago time did not know how to explain this theory as well as boys and girls can today. But he wanted to teach something by having Svetakatu do this experiment. What was it the father wanted to help Svetakatu understand?
- (Again the children may be asked to name real things in the world that cannot be seen.) In how many places can you find something invisible? Name a place where you are sure there is nothing invisible. Svetakatu's father thought that God was made up of all the invisible things in the world. He thought that the Life in us is God and the Life in everything else is God. He believed that God is not far away but an invisible part of our world. That invisible part is everywhere; therefore, God is everywhere.
- (Let the children know that there are at least two different ways of thinking of God.) There are people who think of God as being *above* the world—in the sky. They think that in some way God can look down on everything and everybody on the earth, that God can hear everything and know everything, but they do not think of God as being *in* everything everywhere. They think that God, in the first place, *made* the world and everything else. They call God the Creator, but now that the world has been made, these people

believe God comes down to the earth only once in a while to change the way things are going on.

Perhaps God can be *both* the Life in everything and the Creator of everything. What do you think?

13. The Questions of King Milinda

Most children at some stage in their development are such inveterate askers of questions that they will be intrigued by King Milinda.

It is not a common or advisable idea to interrupt storytelling by asking questions, but this story can be an exception. After giving the introductory part of this story and starting King Milinda off on his journey to find Nagasena, you might stop and ask this question: Can you imagine one of the questions that King Milinda wanted so badly to have answered that he was willing to go on this long journey to find out the answer? Note the children's suggestions, but do not stop to answer their questions. You can return to them later.

When you resume the story and the children discover what King Milinda actually asked, they are likely to be surprised. Perhaps they, too, will be inclined to laugh. Don't allow this to discourage you and don't reprove the laughing. Instead, when the story is finished, give an opportunity for discussion.

Questions

- Has anyone ever seen the really, REAL you?
- Are you invisible?

Wonders of Birth and Mysteries of Death

14. The Birth of Jesus
15. The Birth of Buddha
16. The Birth of Confucius

Although these three stories are in the middle of *From Long Ago and Many Lands*, they could be most appropriately told during the Christmas season.

These three stories should be treated as a unit, even though you may not tell all three in one day. The stories of Buddha and Confucius are included with the story of Jesus so that children in our Christian and Jewish culture may have some background when thinking about the factual truth of Jesus' birth. A similar opportunity for comparison can be given to children in Buddhist and Confucian groups. Children seven years and older can be told how such stories of great men were widely believed after their deaths.

If the children are already familiar with biological facts regarding normal conception and birth, they will comprehend how wonderful and mysterious such miraculous and heralded births could be. They will also appreciate why people of long ago, who knew much less about the human body than we do today, felt differently and needed to let their imaginations weave fanciful tales of angels or dragons or white elephants or other miraculous beings to express their wonder.

These stories present a nice opportunity for comparisons. In "The Birth of Jesus" an angel announces his coming birth. In "The Birth of Buddha" a white elephant does the same, and in "The Birth of Confucius" it is a unicorn that is the heavenly messenger. In the story of Jesus angels sing on the night of his birth. In the story of Buddha sky music is heard, and in the story of Confucius immortals from five planets play on musical instruments while a dragon appears in the sky. Cyrus Baldridge's drawings will help the children to see these parallels.

All these comparisons will give striking evidence that people with imagination, coming from different countries, paint ideas differently. Each artist introduces symbols that are meaningful to him or her. Some like angels as symbols.

Others prefer dragons and unicorns. To others, both angels and dragons seem foolish and are absent from the stories they tell.

It may help the children understand how legends have grown through the ages if you remind them that there are American legends about Washington and Lincoln. An illustration of such a legend is the story of Washington and the cherry tree.

In telling these stories you should foster reverence for life and for great personalities, while letting the children recognize the myths for what they are. Myths need not be seen as untruths but as imaginative responses to religious questions.

Finally, each child could celebrate their birth by bringing in pictures and telling stories about themselves. A reading of "Each Night a Child Is Born Is a Holy Night," by Sophia Lyon Fahs, would be a wonderful closing to this unit.

Questions

- Can you name some things in the three birth stories that are similar and some that are different?
- Can you share some stories about your birth, adoption or entrance into the world? (Help them make the analogy between their stories and the stories of Jesus, Buddha and Confucius.)
- What else do you know about Jesus, Buddha and Confucius?

17. The Mustard-Seed Medicine

This story and the next two stories deal with the mysteries of death. "The Mustard-Seed Medicine" and "A Musician and His Trumpet" are from the very ancient Upanishads of India. "The Road to Olelpanti" is from the Wintu Indians of North America.

Lin Yutang, a well-known Chinese writer, refers to "The Mustard-Seed Medicine" as the most beautiful story from the ancient East.

You might think it is too sad for a young child, but seven

to nine year olds, who are normally secure in their own family relationships, can accept this challenging experience and develop courage from it. Other stories in this book have dealt with the subject of death. Death is an experience that every child has met and wondered about in some form before his or her seventh birthday.

This story portrays death as something that occurs naturally to everyone at some time in their lives and consequently can be accepted without panic. Nothing is more comforting than facing death with a circle of friends who understand from their own experience. Buddha was such a friend to Kisa Gotami. His way of teaching her was gentle and he led her to learn for herself. Through a discussion period for this story, children may discover the extraordinary value of Buddha's way of teaching.

Questions

- Why did Buddha send Kisa Gotami to find the mustard seed?
- How did Kisa Gotami learn to comfort herself?

18. A Musician and His Trumpet

The Aryan people who invaded India sometime between 1,000 and 1 BCE had among them a group of philosophically minded men, who struggled with the great problems of life and death, reality and personality. These men traveled by foot from one important center to another and gathered students about them for the purpose of discussions. Even in India today peasants who can neither read nor write still have their philosophical discussions. All Hindu India has been profoundly influenced by this ancient philosophy.

What is most surprising is that simple stories like "A Musician and His Trumpet" can be found in this philosophical literature. These stories deal with the very same questions that small children puzzle over, and provide answers with the same concrete simplicity.

Before telling this story, ask the children to answer the first three questions so they can talk about their experiences with the death of a pet. After this discussion, tell the children that you will tell a story that was told nearly two thousand years ago. Back then there were people who wondered and puzzled over the same questions the children were thinking about, and a certain man named Kassapa (Kas-sa'-pa) tried to put his ideas into a story.

After the story is told, the last question may help the children to think about its theme.

Questions

- Have you ever had a pet that died?
- How did you feel? Did you wonder about it and wish someone could tell you what you wanted to know?
- What was different about your pet after it had died?
- How would you say, in your own words, what Kassapa meant to say about what happens when a person's body dies?

19. The Road to Olelpanti
This story is from the Wintu Indians who lived long ago at the north tip of present-day California in the Trinity River Valley, near the Pacific Ocean and Mount Shasta. Like many Native American tribes, the Wintu thought the coyote was the most human animal and especially clever. Olebis means "the-great-one-who-sits-above-the-sky."

Questions

- What would the world be like if nobody died? Or animals never died? Or trees and plants never died?
- What did Olebis mean when he said that through "the gladness of birth" and the "sorrow of death" people will come to know love?

Human Universals

Ideals

20. The Complaint Against the Stomach (Ideal: Cooperation)

This story is one of the well-known fables attributed to Aesop of Greece, who lived from about 620 to 560 BCE. It suggests in a very interesting way how much cooperation is continually taking place between the different parts of our bodies without our knowing what is going on.

After telling the story, begin with a "let's suppose" game. The children will be quick to respond with a chain of results. Ask, "Let's suppose your nose stopped working. What would happen? When you become sick, and your throat becomes too sore to swallow, what happens?" Continue as long as the children are interested. It is worthwhile spending time on such a discussion if it helps the children appreciate the amazing cooperative character of the human body.

You may find it helpful to read what Paul said long ago in I Corinthians 12:20-26. He thought that the people in a church or meeting are like one body. Use one of the modern versions or simplify the language for the children.

The children may find this story amusing but you might foster some thoughts about the need for a world community.

After such a discussion, you can foster the children's imaginations by asking questions about other things where the different parts are very important to the good of the whole.

Questions

- Suppose your parent(s) stopped cooking? Suppose your mother or father stopped going to work? Suppose one of the children had a tantrum?
- Suppose the sanitation person stopped collecting the garbage? Or the mailperson refused to deliver the mail?
- Would you say that a family is like a person's body? Would you say a city is like a person's body?
- Who are the most important people? Or is everyone important? How should we treat one another?

21. The Trees Choose a King (Ideal: Democracy)

This story is probably as old as the Jataka tales. It is one of the oldest stories in the Bible. The children should know that the Bible is a collection of some very old books that were written by people living in Palestine who are now called Jews. The original rendering of this story can be found in the Hebrew Bible, Judges 9:1-15.

This story is an opportunity to highlight many of the values in a democracy: the privilege of serving, the obligations and sacrifices involved in accepting an office and the thoughtful choice of officers.

Even an eight year old can realize when she or he should sometimes sacrifice her or his time and personal wishes to help a group. This realization may come when they're working out some class project that involves team effort.

If the class is mature enough, it would be a good experience in democracy to elect a member of the class to some duty in the religious education program or congregation. If this is done, the office should be treated with respect and be given opportunities to report. To impress the group and to give a number of children the opportunity to serve, there should be a frequent turnover of office.

Questions

- Why did the olive tree refuse the kingship?
- If you had been one of the trees, would you have chosen the thorn bush to be your king?
- What would you expect of a leader?
- What makes people accept an office? What makes some people refuse an office?

22. A Visit to the Land-of-Great-Men (Ideal: Sincerity)

This is a very old story taken from one of China's great books called the *Ching Hau Yuan*, written over a thousand years ago. The book is similar to a Chinese *Gulliver's Travels*. It is a fanciful dream, but one that had a serious impact on life in its day.

Introduce the story by asking the children about their own wishes and dreams: Has anyone ever made up a story in which you imagined that things were different and better then they really are? Have you made up a story of how one of your wishes came true?

After telling the story, the children might play imaginatively for a while with this idea of having a cloud that would always tell the truth about their feelings. What difference would it make to them? Would they like that kind of a country? Why not? Why did the plan work so well in this story?

Questions

- Without the help of clouds, how can people discover each other's feelings?
- What kinds of "red silk" do people sometimes use to hide the colors of their "clouds"?
- What does the word "sincerity" mean? Give examples.
- Is there someone who always knows just how you are feeling? Who is it? (Some children may say they believe there is a God who always knows. Others may believe it is only themselves who will know. Some may say both.)
- Can we fool ourselves?

23. The Whale and the Big Bronze Statue (Ideal: Greatness)
This is a story to be enjoyed and not taken too seriously. In a humorous way it challenges the idea that being big is the same as being important. The statue of Buddha was six inches shorter than the whale, but which was more important, the real Buddha or the whale?

If possible, obtain a photograph of this statue. It stands on a platform shaped in a lotus flower in a place called Kamakura. It is a one-hour train ride from Yokohama. Often referred to as the *Diabutsu* or Great Buddha, this statue can be compared in size to the Statue of Liberty. It towers approximately fifty feet above its base. Help the children to imagine how high fifty feet is. Buddha's face alone is longer than the tallest person any of the children have ever seen—between eight and nine feet long. One of his ears is as long as a baby's body. The small round silver ball on his forehead is a foot across. Your entire class could probably squeeze into the palms of his hands. It is indeed a very big statue.

Whales are also very big. Perhaps one of the children will be interested in finding out how big whales grow.

Questions

- Have you ever heard people brag about something being the biggest thing in the world? Name some of these things. Seven hundred years ago, when this statue of Buddha was made, do you suppose people bragged about it? What do you suppose the person who made up this story was thinking about? What was he or she trying to say with this story?
- How much does being big matter? Who was the bigger and taller man, Washington or Lincoln? (Name other well-known people.) How much does their size have to do with their greatness?
- What do we look for in a friend? His or her size?
- (Close the discussion by thinking about some very small things.) Are any small things more important than these big things we have talked about? (See how many tiny but very important things the children can name.)

Realities

24. The Nervous Little Rabbit (Reality: Fear)
This is one of the famous Jataka or Birth Stories from India. There are 550 Jataka tales. These fables are popularly known as stories told by Buddha about his own experiences in his former incarnations. Many of the stories are doubtless much older than him. After Buddha's death, the fables were collected together with stories the Buddha actually told and all were linked with his name. This story, "The Nervous Little Rabbit," probably dates back to a time before 563 BCE when Buddha is thought to have been born.

Although young children will not be interested in all the information given above, they will like to know that this story, and others that they are going to hear, are in the oldest storybook in the world and that this book was written in India. Their imaginations will grow as they try to think of the thousands and thousands of girls and boys who already have heard this story. In sharing this knowledge, you have an opportunity to foster feelings of being a part of one world. The proverb "Under the sky all are one family" (see endpapers) might be written on newsprint where the children can read it often. Show the children how it is written in many languages on the end papers.

Questions

- What mistake did the "nervous little rabbit" make?
- Do we ever make mistakes like that? Give examples.
- What are the dangers that may occur when we hand on uncertain knowledge?
- What does "rumor" mean? (Play the "rumor game." Whisper a sentence to the child next to you. Let him or her whisper it to his or her neighbor. Continue to the last child who says aloud what he or she has understood to be whispered in his or her ear. Compare it with the original sentence.)
- What harm can spreading rumors do?
- How did the rabbit finally get rid of her fear?

25. The Miller, His Boy and Their Donkey
(Reality: Indecision)
This story is from the well-known fables attributed to Aesop of Greece, who lived from about 620 to 560 BCE. The children need to realize that it is a fairy tale, told because the storyteller wanted to say something.

Questions

- What did the storyteller want to say?
- Did he mean to say that one should never listen to the advice of another person?
- Did he mean to say that one should listen to, but *not follow*, the advice of another person? What did he mean? How should one decide on what to do?
- What should the miller have done instead of what he did?
- Perhaps you will hear someone say to someone else, "You are carrying the donkey." Can you guess what that phrase means?

26. The Wee, Wise Bird (Reality: Mistakes)

This story is an old rabbinical tale, which may be difficult for children this age to understand. Ask if they have any questions. To help them comprehend its meaning, review the three pieces of advice that the "wee, wise bird" gave the gardener:

- Never cry over spilt milk.
- Do not wish for something you know cannot be had.
- Do not believe what you know cannot possibly be true.

Make sure the children know what each one means.

Questions

- Did the gardener cry over spilt milk? What was he wishing for that he knew he could not have?
- What did the gardener believe that he should have known could not possibly be true?
- What are some things that we cannot have but foolishly wish for?
- How can we be sure something is impossible?
- Have some people succeeded in making things happen that seemed impossible to most people? Give examples.
- Can you think of certain things that some people believe and that you are sure cannot possibly be true?

- Would you call this bird "a wee, wise bird" or not?

27. Who Ate the Squabs? (Reality: Dishonesty)
This story comes from Czechoslovakia, but similar stories are found in many cultures and countries.

It is fortunate that this story about dishonesty is so humorous. Our culture tends to exaggerate the sin of lying. Mutual trust, dependability and frankness are basic virtues, but, strange as it may seem, the more we seek honesty from children through praise and blame, the more difficult we make its attainment. The need to cover up the truth is usually a result of fear of condemnation or the loss of affection and approval.

Let the children know that it is a universal human trait to be afraid of letting people know the truth about ourselves. Almost everyone at one time or another has told a lie. We often pretend to be better than we really are. Laugh over the story of the squabs and tell of a time when you yourself did something and were too ashamed to admit the truth.

Encourage the children to think of better solutions than the one the shoemaker and his wife found.

Questions

- How could the husband have helped the wife?
- How could the wife have helped the husband?

28. The Two Cheats (Reality: Cheating)
This story is from long ago Uganda. The country has changed radically and bark cloth is not often used for clothes today. But it is used for wall hangings and decorative purposes. Fried ants are still eaten and are regarded as a delicacy. If you can find samples of bark cloth or decorative bark hangings, it would enhance this story. Pictures would be helpful, too.

There is great humor in this story. Each cheat gets caught in the same way he wanted to catch the other. Ask the children if they feel sorry for either one.

Questions

- What do you think about cheating when you don't get caught? Does that happen? Is anybody hurt then? Who?
- What are some of the ways people in our country cheat? Do children ever cheat? How? What does one gain by cheating? What does one lose?

29. The Old Bowl (Reality: Greed)

This story is one of the five hundred fifty Jataka tales from ancient India supposedly told by Buddha himself. If possible remind the children through pictures of the people who live and lived in India.

Questions

- Does the second peddler, Seriva, remind you of anyone you have known or heard? (Hopefully, the children will mention people in various walks of life.) If so, isn't it clear that excellent character has nothing to do with occupation? A person may have a menial job and be a superior man or woman. A cook, a grocer, a mailperson and a doctor may be equally deserving of respect and admiration.
- How was the greedy peddler punished? Suppose the second peddler, Seriva, had not come along just in time, what would have happened?
- Which parts of the story give you the happiest feelings? When the first peddler was punished? Or when the grandmother and girl were given enough to live on for a while? Or when the second peddler was able to sell the bowl for a lot of money?

Human Diversity

The following eight stories enhance the theme of the endpapers, "Under the sky, all people are one family," which says YES we are all alike, and YES we are all different.

These stories affirm the uniqueness of every individual and value human diversity. They celebrate all people as members of the human family with the same needs and rights.

30. The Blind Men and the Elephant

This story is from India and supposedly told by Buddha when his monks were debating their beliefs and answers to life's universal questions. The humor in this story will appeal to children, who will enjoy the absurdity of the quarrel and the stubbornness of the blind men.

Children may like to role play the story or play a game patterned after this story. Let them create an imaginary animal, or use some large object and let a blindfolded group feel only a part of the animal or object, and guess what it is.

Questions

- Can you think of people you know who were too sure they were right about something when they really knew very little about it? Tell us.
- Can you think about some of the things we may never know for sure?

31. The Ring-around of Temper

This story comes from present-day Thailand, ancient Burma. The cumulative structure of this story has always fascinated children, which is similar to *The House That Jack Built* or *The Big Turnip*.

When a person is hurt, it seems quite natural for him or her to want to hurt back. Children will agree they have often felt this way. It is a bothersome situation for anybody. The people and animals in this story did strike back. Why didn't it work? What was wrong with what they did?

In such a discussion, it is probably wise for you to stick to the main point of the story. Explain that when we become cross or angry, we frequently take out our feelings on someone who is not to blame at all. Ask the children for good ways to snap out of their anger.

Do not encourage children to cover up emotions behind a mask. Above all else, encourage children to be honest with themselves and with you.

Because this is another story that deals with deep emotions, free art work is likely to be a better medium of expression than talk. Suggest that the children paint pictures of times when they have felt cross or angry or wanted to hit. Reassure them that everyone feels that way once in a while. Some children may like to add a picture of what they did do or wish they had done when angry.

When discussing the pictures or talking about what to do, help the children understand that it is important to listen to the other person and to stop and think.

Questions

- What made Chem do this to the nearby tree?
- Did he mean to do it? Or was it an accident? Or was he feeling cross at somebody else and took it out on the tree?
- The people and the animals in this story did strike back. Why didn't it work? What was wrong with what they did?

32. The Blind Man and the Lame Man

This short story is from Uganda but similar stories have been told in many different countries around the world. Such a story of mutual helpfulness between a person who is blind and a person who is lame seems to be a universal favorite.

The straightforwardness of the story is clear and needs no elaboration. Engage the children in discussing the two men, the incidents and the "case of the quits." Invite them to share similar experiences of helpfulness between children of special needs or between the members of a family.

Questions

- Why did these two men need to leave their village?
- What does "a case of the quits" mean?

33. The Two Friends

This is another Jataka tale from ancient India. It is a simple animal story that is likely to involve some natural conversation about animal pets.

Questions

- Have you ever had an animal that missed you when you were away? Or missed its baby when it was taken away? How did the animal act?
- Have you ever missed someone very much? How did you feel? How did you feel when that person came back to you?
- This story is thought to be one that Buddha told long, long ago. From this story, what would you guess about the way Buddha felt toward animals?
- Do you suppose that some animals think and feel? What experiences have you had to make you think so?

34. King Saul Finds a Harpist

This story is from the Hebrew scriptures, I Samuel 16:14-23 and 18:1-29. This is the first of three stories about Saul; the stories belong together but can be told separately or all together.

Questions

- Why do you think Saul threw the spear?

- Name one of the reasons for Saul's illness. What kind of "soothing" music did David play to help quiet Saul? Do you know the most soothing music in the world? (Invite them to share their experiences with lullabies.)
- (Name one of the reasons for Saul's illness as jealousy. Define jealousy as when we are afraid that a person is better than we are or will take something away from us that we want to keep. Share one of your experiences with jealousy. Highlight these facts when asking the following questions.)

  a. David moved to the palace and lived with King Saul and became friends with Saul's children, especially Jonathan.
  b. David and Jonathan played together and worked together. What kind of work did they do? What work did Jonathan do before he came to the palace?
  c. David and Jonathan became good friends. Was Jonathan Saul's friend, too? Explain some of the dynamics of their relationship.

- The people in Saul's kingdom so loved and praised David that the poor, sick Saul thought: "They think more of David than they do of me. They will make him king in my place. If I do not get rid of David, I shall lose my kingdom." At first King Saul thought that he could control David if David became his son-in-law. His sick thoughts grew even stronger and it was then that he tried to kill David. He must have suffered terribly before he threw that spear.

  None of us likes to be left out. We want people to like us and be our friends. Sometimes we can't get noticed by being pleasant, so we try by being bad. Has that ever happened to you? Often when we are angry with other people it is really because we are unhappy with ourselves. Would Saul have been happier if he could have stayed friends with David?

35. David and Jonathan Become Friends

This is the second story in the series of Saul stories and can be found in the Hebrew scriptures of the Bible, I Samuel 19:1-10 and 20:1-42.

Questions

- David and Jonathan are often spoken of as the world's most famous friends. Do you see anything remarkable about the way Jonathan treated David? Or about the way David treated Jonathan?
- Is there anything in the story that doesn't seem right or that bothers you? (Perhaps someone will be bothered by the lie that both David and Jonathan planned to tell King Saul.) Was this lie needed? Can you think of how it could have been avoided?
- Do you have a best friend? Why do you call her or him your best friend? How do you treat her or him and how does she or he treat you?

36. King Saul's Spear and Water Jug

This is the third of the Saul stories and can be found in the Bible's Hebrew scriptures, I Samuel 22:1-2 and 26:1-25. This third story is suspenseful and adds more details to the picture of these two famous friends.

Questions

- Were you expecting David to do what he did? What did you expect?
- Would it have been better if he had killed Saul? If not, why not?
- (Even though the children will not use the big word "magnanimity", they will have a feeling for its meaning after hearing this story.) What do you think about the motto "an eye for an eye," or revenge or forgiveness? (Keep the discussion at their level.)

37. Damon and Pythias

This story can be found in *Parallel Lives,* written by Plutarch, a great Greek biographer who lived from about 46 to 125 BCE. This version of the story was written by Florence W. Klabler in 1948 for the original edition of *From Long Ago and Many Lands.*

Damon and Pythias, like David and Jonathan, have long been an example of two ideal friends. It seems that people the world over admire people who know how to be friends.

Questions

- (Encourage the children to talk about the two men.) What do you admire in Pythias? What unusual things did he do?
     (Two things are outstanding. First, Pythias was not afraid to speak out and say what he thought was wrong about the things the Governor was doing even though he knew this might bring a death sentence upon him. Second, he thought of his parents and what they would need after his death instead of merely being frightened over his own dying; Pythias was loyal and not only to his close friend.)
- What was unusual or admirable about what Damon did? Why was Damon willing to risk his own life in the way he did? (Help the children to see that it was not only because he loved his friend Pythias and wanted to do him a kindness, but because he completely trusted his friend's word.)
- If two people are to be friends, how important is it for both of them to speak the truth and stand by their word? (Perhaps the word "trust" may have new meaning for the children as a result of this discussion.)

38. The Camel Driver in Need of a Friend

This story is from the Arabs, followers of the Islamic religion. When this story was first told they may have been living in Arabia.

Before telling the story say, "This story may remind you of Damon and Pythias, but there is an important difference.

See if you can find it." Probably no further questioning will be needed, but if some stimulus is called for, the following questions may be useful.

Questions

- Suppose you were in this crowd, heard the story of what the camel driver had done and been told that he was to be killed. Would you have tried to help him?
- What do you think about the camel driver? Would you have trusted his word? Why? Why not? How do you explain Abu Dhur's willingness to act as "surety" for him? Do you think that Abu Khur did anything different from what Damon did? Which was harder to do?
- Were you expecting the Caliph to do what he did? How did you like his decision?

39. Wise King Solomon

This story is from the Hebrew scriptures of the Bible and can be found in I Kings 3:4-28. There are two themes in this famous story: (a) dreams and wishes and (b) mothers and babies.

A lead-in activity to this story may enhance its meaning for the children. You could ask them to draw or paint a picture of something they wish for most. After these pictures are finished, invite the children to share, compare and contrast their wishes.

The story about the two babies and the two mothers deserves a treatment of its own. It was told to show that King Solomon was wise.

Questions

- What was wise about what King Solomon did?
- Do you think that King Solomon expected the baby to be cut in two? Why then did he command that a sword be brought?

- Do you suppose King Solomon noticed any differences between the two women that made him suspect who was not the real mother? What might he have noticed?
- What kind of mother do you like best?

40. Jesus at a Wedding Party

This story is found in the Christian scriptures of the Bible, Luke 6:32-36 and 14:7-14. Although the people at the party were all adults, invite the children to comment on their behavior.

Questions

- What was Jesus' idea about choosing people to invite to parties?
- How would his idea work if you gave a party?
- Parties are meant for fun, but sometimes they can hurt people. How would you feel if you were the only person in your class not invited to a party to which everyone else was going?
- Picture yourself as a child left out of a party because your color, race or religion were different from those of the other children. How would you feel? (This story is a good opportunity to talk about parties: the obligations of the host and guests. Because this is a serious question in children's social life, spend some thought and time on it.)

41. The Richest Man in the World

This story is a Greek historical legend and can be found in the works of Herodotus, who lived in the fifth century BCE. Solon was the ruler of Athens and Croesus was king of Lydia in Asia Minor. Both of these rulers lived at the time of Cyrus the Great, who ruled during the sixth century BCE.

The story raises two questions: Who are the happiest people in the world? And what are the most beautiful things in the world? Introduce the story by posing two questions for the children:

- What is the most beautiful thing you have seen this past week? (Write their list of things on newsprint.)
- Who is the happiest person you know? (Invite sharing.)

Read or tell the story. Then ask the children what they think of Solon's remarks.

Encourage the children to criticize Solon's remarks. Perhaps he was mistaken. Riches in themselves do not make a person happy, yet having useful and beautiful things that money can buy may increase happiness. More criminals come out of poverty-stricken homes than come from homes where a comfortable living is possible. Do not belittle the value of the things that money can buy.

Questions

- Which is easier—to be happy without much money to live on, or to be happy when you have all the pretty and useful things you want?
- What was wrong with King Croesus' thinking? Perhaps he wanted to be happier than anyone else, and he thought that if he was richer than anyone else he would be happier. What was wrong about that? (Let the children wonder and question instead of emphasizing a moral.)

42. The Wind and the Sun

This story is one of Aesop's fables. Aesop lived in Greece from about 620 to 560 BCE. This fable asks, Who or what is the strongest?

Questions

- Aesop, who was said to have told this story about the wind and sun, wanted to remind us of other things that are like the wind and sun. What do you suppose Aesop was thinking of?
- Can you think of anything besides the sun that is very strong

and powerful but makes no noise at all? What are they?

- Did you ever try to do something in a blustering, noisy way, a little like the wind? Tell us about it. Did it work?
- What does this story seem to mean? Does this idea remind you of any other story we have already heard? (It will be significant if someone recalls King Asoka's thought about kindness. You can write his words again on newsprint: "The only true conquest is that which is brought about by kindness. . . . Let this Law of Life be remembered as long as there are a sun and moon in the sky.")
- What are some things that can be accomplished by kindness? What is accomplished by being rough and tough?

תַּחוֹת שְׁמַיָּא כָּל־בְּנֵי אֲנָשָׁא מִשְׁפָּחָה חֲדָה

Sotto il cielo siamo tutti una sola famiglia

Unter dem Himmel sind wir alle eine Familie

जन कुल पेक पेव

DEBAIXO DO CEU
TODOS SÃO
UMA SÓ FAMÍLIA

天 下 一 家

תַּחַת הַשָּׁמַיִם כָּל־אָדָם אֶחָד

زیر آسمان ایک خاندان